Every coin tells a story. Some coins tell us about kings and queens, presidents, or even gods and goddesses; others tell us about famous explorers, historic discoveries, or wild animals. With this book, you can begin building your own collection of fascinating coins from around the world.

The coins shown above come from Israel, India, Uruguay, Sri Lanka, and the Philippines. These are just a few of the many beautiful coin designs from around the world. This book will tell you how to find collectible coins on a beginner's budget, and what to look for when you find them.

START COLLECTING

COINS

Margo Russell

RUNNING PRESS
PHILADELPHIA · LONDON

9 8 7 6 5 4 3 2 1
Digit on the right indicates the number of this printing

Library of Congress Cataloging-in-Publication Number 96-67145

ISBN 1-56138-762-2

Cover and poster design by Diane Miljat

The author wishes to thank Jay Guren of *Coin World* for looking at the manuscript
and honing out typos and any thoughts that dangled.

Photographs: Pages 25, 28 (top and middle left), 29, 30 (bottom), 73 (top), 82, courtesy American Numismatic Society.
Pages 27, 30 (top), 35, courtesy Ashmolean Museum. Pages 11, 13, 23, 26, 28 (bottom left), 34, 36, 39 (top), courtesy
Bettmann Archives. Page 52, courtesy British Royal Mint. Pages 86, 87, copyright Coin World. Used by permission.
Page 38, courtesy Independence National Historical Park Collection. Pages 15, 18–22, 95, courtesy Michael Kolman.
Pages 81, 83 (top), 84, courtesy Professional Numismatics Guild, Inc. Pages 88–91, courtesy Royal Canadian Mint.
Pages 31, 32, courtesy Smithsonian Institution, National Museum of American History, numismatic division.
Page 74, courtesy United States Department of Interior, National Park Service, Saint-Gaudens National Historic
Site, Cornish, New Hampshire. Pages 42, 65, 66, 67, 68, 71, 75 (bottom), 77, courtesy United States Mint.
Photograph of Margo Russell courtesy Armand Champa.

This book may be ordered by mail from the publisher. Please include $2.50 for postage and handling.
But try your bookstore first!

Running Press Book Publishers
125 South Twenty-second Street
Philadelphia, Pennsylvania 19103-4399

To coin collectors

past, present, and future

CONTENTS

INTRODUCTION

Coin collecting is exciting, educational, friendly, and fun—and more than 2,000 years old! There has to be something special about a hobby that stands such a test of time to be enjoyed to this very day.

However, the ancient Romans, who collected Greek coins for their beauty thousands of years ago, would find it hard to believe how one of the world's greatest hobbies has progressed. Now there are thousands of coins with fascinating designs to collect from around the world, from ancient coins to the modern, action-packed gold and silver Olympic Centennial series. Coin prices range from almost nothing (the change in your pocket or dresser drawer) to millions of dollars.

Coin collectors have never known boundaries, but there is new excitement in this world-class hobby as collectors advance toward the 21st century and the computer age. Technology has helped create an explosion of worldwide collector-to-collector coin talk. Collectors use e-mail and faxes to communicate. They research indexes, directories, books, and encyclopedias, check coin prices, and buy and sell with their computers.

How does one start collecting? First, remember, everybody in the hobby was once a beginner. And you don't need a computer. One 11-year-old collector we know began by asking questions and building a library of coin books. Only now is he relating the hobby to his computer. His family is supportive and sees that he attends coin events and conventions. Many adult friends have helped him. That's another bonus of collecting—coin friends can be friends for life. Their common interests create a special bonding. Many coin dealers are helpful and will guide new collectors.

Never in coin collecting history have there been more ways to learn about coins. Actually it's an information explosion. Famous Broadway and Hollywood stars have narrated coin videos and movies. How-to cassettes, slide sets, and correspondence courses are readily available.

There are coin club meetings, seminars, conferences, conventions for all ages, and even a national coin week to spread the word about the hobby. There are coin museums to browse and general and specialized coin books, beautifully illustrated, that are collector's items themselves. There are weekly newspapers and monthly magazines just for coin collectors.

Teachers know that the study of coins can enhance knowledge of history, mathematics, art, archeology, geography, language, and science. The United States Treasury Department, the United States Mint, and the Bureau of Printing and Engraving recognize the importance of coins to education and have developed "The Money Story," an excellent video and curriculum guide. (See ordering details on page 105.)

Surely those Romans who first collected coins centuries ago would be amazed at today's rich resources for the enjoyment of coin collecting. And that's what it's all about—enjoyment!

Chapter 1

THE TIMELESS HOBBY

We know that more than 2,000 years ago coins were collected for themselves, quite apart from their practical use to buy and sell goods and services. It is believed wealthy Greeks appreciated and set aside their own beautiful coins to admire. We know that Aristotle and Plato were aware of the importance of coins and their impact on the economy. The Romans admired and collected Greek coins as well as their own. Ancient writers such as Pliny, Plutarch, and Cicero could not have ignored coins as they wrote about the art and treasure of their time.

It's said that money talks. It's true. No, it doesn't speak out loud, but coins tell fascinating, accurate stories of human history. Because coins are made of indestructible metals, and because people value and protect them, they last for centuries, furnishing us

The ancient Greeks produced and collected beautiful coins like this one. The obverse (front) depicts the mythical figure Arethusa surrounded by dolphins; the reverse (back) shows Nike, the goddess of victory, crowning a charioteer.

obverse

date

designer's initials

design

mint mark

Coins are full of information—if you know where to look. This $5 gold half eagle, minted to commemorate the Statue of Liberty, is marked to show the names collectors use for the parts of a coin.

with a literal time-line of civilization. When we begin to collect and examine coins, the past comes alive as we study the pieces.

Collectible coins are not confined to old specimens. The United States Mint recognizes the importance of coins and collectors. Its

reverse

legend

motto

rim

customer service branch handles the sale of beautiful new coins by mail and over the counter at the Philadelphia and Denver mints and the Old Mint Museum in San Francisco. Many world mints offer the same service.

CONTEMPORARY COLLECTORS

Today there are more coins to collect than ever before, and thousands of collectors around the world. Coin collectors know no boundaries. It is said that the hobby creates such a bond between collectors that if it were up to them, there would be only friendship and peace in the world.

Designed for Queen Victoria, this 1839 gold pattern is one of the finest examples of coinage art. The reverse depicts the queen as "Truth" guiding a lion, the symbol of power.

Organizations of dedicated collectors at every level—international, national, regional, and local—meet regularly and hold conventions to exchange information, to learn, to enjoy contacts with other collectors, and to trade, buy, and sell coins.

Museums all over the world house collections of coins. The three most important in the United States are the American Numismatic Society in New York, the numismatic wing of the Smithsonian Institution's National Museum of American History in Washington, D.C., and the American Numismatic Association in Colorado Springs.

Collectors believe strongly that one must learn about coins as well as collect them. They have a saying: "First the book and then the coin."

Some libraries specialize in books on coins and money. The American Numismatic Society's research library is said to be the finest of these in the world. Members may borrow books by mail from the American Numismatic Association. Every year, updated standard references and almanacs on coins are published.

You will also find exciting new books about coins. Some of them even read like novels, such as *Adventures with Rare Coins* by Q. David Bowers, former president of the American Numismatic Association. (For more books about coins, see pp. 102.)

Coin slide and video presentations have been developed by collector organizations and by commercial firms. Weekly newspapers and monthly magazines for collectors report the latest happenings in the hobby and

These sunken treasures found off the Florida coast include Spanish pieces-of-eight, a popular coin of the pirate days. Deep-sea treasure finds often yield interesting coins for collectors.

contain feature articles to stimulate collecting. Exciting deep-sea treasure finds and multimillion-dollar coin auctions make headlines in the national press.

Collectors have another motto: "Never say never about a coin!" Tomorrow there may be a new discovery or new information about a known piece to change its history or its pedigree. That's part of the excitement.

Coin collectors are outgoing, friendly, and always willing to share their knowledge and the joys of their hobby. Young people in particular receive attention and encouragement so that they can learn for themselves how much they can gain in fun, satisfaction, and (in many cases) future profit. Adult coin clubs consider it a responsibility to plan activities for junior members.

YOUNG COLLECTORS

Young collectors have their own clubs and coin publications. There are events where they can exhibit their collections and win prizes. Auctions are offered specifically for young people, where they can bid spiritedly on affordable coins. National educational seminars, usually held in the summer, teach the basics of collecting. The Boy Scouts of America have a coin collecting merit badge and study manual.

The Treasury Department distributes classroom aids to further coin knowledge. Many teachers use coins as instruction tools. Coin collecting offers a pleasant way to learn about history, geography, economics, archaeology, architecture, art, chemistry, engineering, and metallurgy. Coins have been recommended for blind students, who can learn a great deal by studying the raised surfaces with their fingers.

THE SCIENCE OF COLLECTING COINS

The study of money is not just a hobby; it is a learned science. The study of coins and objects used as money has become so important as a discipline that a science called numismatics (noo-miz-MAT-iks) has developed over the years. Taken from the Greek word for coin (*nomisma*), numismatics is defined as the study, science, and collecting of coins, medals, paper money, tokens, and similar objects.

Numismatic studies are offered in North America at the university level and in seminars for graduate students. Some major European universities have numismatic chairs.

Numismatic scholars share their research and knowledge through books, papers, lectures, and conferences. Archaeological digs often produce new coins and other objects for numismatists to study.

"Spade" money from ancient China, produced during the Chou Dynasty (1064–722 B.C.), is one of the earliest known types of metal coins.

COIN DEALERS

In addition to collectors and numismatic scholars, a third group has evolved from coin collecting—professional coin dealers. Many fine numismatists have chosen to become dealers. They earn a good living while enjoying their hobby and their contacts with customers. Dealers serve an important function. They provide a marketplace where coins are bought and sold in shops, by mail, at conventions, and during auctions. The richly illustrated coin catalogs on high-quality paper developed for some auctions are considered valuable references and are themselves collected.

A reliable bit of advice for anyone new to the hobby: if you don't know your coins, know your dealer. Some dealers are like walking coin encyclopedias. They like to share their prolific knowledge, both in person and through books. Most dealers will take time to help a newcomer. Some dealers offer boxes and baskets of inexpensive coins in their shops or at coin shows so that new collectors can make purchases.

One collector compares coin collecting to a three-legged stool: one leg represents the hobby; another, the science of numismatists; and the third, the profession. The collector, the scholar, and the dealer support each other and offer many avenues of opportunity to the enthusiast. It is possible to be all three. That's why more and more people are entering the fascinating and diverse world of coin collecting.

Chapter 2

THE EARLIEST MONEY

Can you imagine a world without coins or money as we know it today? Think how many times we use coins in our day-to-day life. How could we make change when we buy food and clothing or pay for services without coins?

Some futurists predict that one day we will become a cashless society and transact all our business electronically. Only time will tell if we will give up our coins.

THE BARTER SYSTEM

Once there was a time when there was no money at all. Our ancient ancestors soon discovered that not everything they needed and wanted could be found in their own backyards. The inland farmer had grain but longed for fish to eat. Meanwhile the fisherman eyed the farmer's wheat and barley. They decided to trade products. This process of exchanging commodities is known as barter, the oldest form of trade.

Soon it became clear that some things were more valuable than others, so a standard value was put on such possessions as camels, oxen, cattle, sheep, and goats. In time, rice, corn, tea, sugar, and other foodstuffs, with salt and pepper added to make them savory, were used for barter.

SHELL MONEY

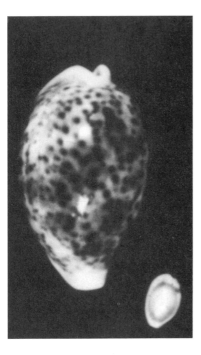

The expression "shell out" refers to one of the earliest forms of money. Cowrie shells, more portable and durable than food and animals, were used as "coins" on every continent. They were readily available, easy to carry, and decorative. One could even flaunt one's wealth by wearing it around the neck. Some cultures attached special powers and even fertility to shells.

The cowrie shell was at one time the most common medium of exchange among primitive people. It was used throughout Africa, Asia, and the islands of the Pacific.

PRIMITIVE MONEY FROM THE NEAR EAST

As early as 2500 B.C. the Egyptians were using rings of gold for money. The rings were weighed for each transaction because they had no marks to designate their worth. Clay and bronze tablets, cubes, bars of gold, and the Old Testament talents and shekels (units of gold and silver) were recognized as objects of value and were used for exchange in the earliest cultures.

 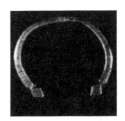

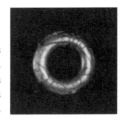 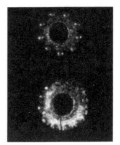

Primitive money in the shape of rings has been found in many parts of the world. The pieces shown here come from India (top left), West Africa (top right), China (bottom left), and Ireland (bottom right).

PRIMITIVE MONEY FROM THE FAR EAST

"Key" money from China, A.D. 650.

The Chinese grew tired of hoisting the heavy knives, spades, hoes, and other tools they were using for barter. Sometime between the seventh and fourth centuries B.C. they made miniatures of these useful objects, first in copper and then in bronze. They also made miniature saddles, trousers, "pants" money (called *pu*), and "knife" money (called *tao*). "Ant nose" money, named because it carried marks resembling ants, looked like cowrie shells.

This beautiful Chinese jade coin, called "jewel of heaven," was believed to bring luck to its owner.

Oriental "money trees" fascinate collectors of primitive money even though it is believed they were not widely used in trade. They appeared in many different shapes and sizes. The coins were mounted on metal "trees" and broken off as needed. The stem or trunk was returned for smelting so a new tree could be cast. Silk was also an Asian commodity, very valuable because it was so difficult to process.

This "frying pan" amulet is from the Han Dynasty, about A.D. 100. The Chinese often made coins in the shape of commonly used objects.

Chinese pu or "pants" money A.D. 350.

Brass Chinese "money tree"—coins were broken off and used as needed.

THE LARGEST "COINS"

In contrast to the practical Chinese, the primitive people of the Island of Yap in the Pacific Ocean made money out of stone—some of it weighing two tons and measuring 12 feet across. Shaped like millstones, Yap money has a hole in the center of each stone for a pole to allow the "coins" to be hoisted and carried around. Smaller versions of Yap stones were used to buy coconuts, canoes, pigs, land, or brides. A few examples of Yap money have been exhibited at museums in the United States.

Stone money from the Island of Yap in the West Pacific. The stones were taken from other islands and carried many miles in small boats. Owners of the larger stones displayed them in front of their homes to demonstrate their wealth.

EARLY AFRICAN MONEY

Early African money is especially fascinating and collectible, although some of it is difficult to locate and preserve. The *kissi* penny is an example of an interesting African coin. It is a thin, pencil-like iron object, ranging from 12 to 24 inches in length, shaped like a wing at one end and a tail at the other. It was believed that the penny's soul would drain out if it were broken, and that only a witch doctor could restore the spirit. It is sometimes called the "money with a soul."

Among the many objects used for trade in early Africa were ivory, needles, iron bars, copper crosses weighing more than two pounds, manillas (partial rings of copper, brass, and sometimes iron), feathers, copper collars and bracelets, ax and spear heads, and miniature spears.

Other cultures created money from the materials at hand, often styling them after objects and animals around them. They used wild boar tusks, fishhooks, beeswax, bamboo, jade, drums, gongs, and bells. They shaped their money like canoes, tiger tongues, and ants. Cultures that depended on the sea used whale, porpoise, and shark teeth for trade. Dog teeth, woodpecker heads, vessels of stone, pottery, and mahogany logs were all used for money.

Handwrought iron "spear" money from Central Africa. The small spear with the copper-wrapped shaft is from the Bakuba tribe.

Dog tooth money from New Guinea. Only the two canine teeth were used, so this necklace represented considerable wealth.

EARLY NATIVE AMERICAN MONEY

Native American shell money with rough etchings is believed to have been used for trading by coastal and inland tribes centuries before the arrival of European settlers. Coinlike coal objects with inscriptions have been found in early Native American burial grounds. The Plains Indians used the tomahawk and the peace pipe for trade.

The Aztecs of Central America used the cocoa bean for small transactions, but for large purchases they used goose quills filled with gold dust. Some early European-American plantation owners formed tobacco into sticks and shipped it to the South Pacific to be used as money.

COLLECTING PRIMITIVE MONEY

Collectors sometimes refer to primitive money as "odd and curious" money. There are organizations specifically for collectors of these early forms of money. Each year, the International Primitive Money Society holds its own meeting as a part of the American Numismatic Association convention. There are also several catalogs published dealing with this fascinating branch of coin collecting. You will find some primitive pieces on the market that are affordable for young collectors, such as the *kissi* penny and shark's tooth money.

This beautifully carved whale tooth was used as money on the Solomon Islands of the West Pacific.

This shark's tooth (left) and harpoon point carved from bone (right) were used for trade by the Eskimos of the Aleutian Islands.

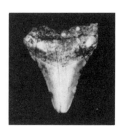

Chapter 3

ANCIENT COINS

> *"All passes. Art alone*
> *Enduring stays to us;*
> *The bust outlasts the throne—*
> *The coin, Tiberius."*
>
> —HENRY AUSTIN DOBSON

Time stands still on coins. Although they were invented as a convenience, the coins of the ancient world have become a form of history books frozen in metal for us today. They have often outlasted the fragile written word and are sometimes the only surviving record of a civilization and its people.

Coin collectors hold in their hands coins that have withstood centuries of dust, rubble, wars, volcanic eruptions, and fallen empires.

Ancient coins often bear portraits of powerful figures, both real and imaginary. This Greek coin depicts King Hiero II of Syracuse (c. 270–216 B.C.). On the reverse, Nike, the goddess of victory, drives a chariot.

We can thank ancient peoples and their custom of burying coins during danger or emergencies for the abundance of ancient coins today. Thousands of coins have been found in hoards over the years. Soldiers buried coins as they marched, hoping to return for them. Families dug deep pits and secreted their coins in jars if an enemy approached. More and more important coin finds are being reported these days, exciting to numismatic scholars, who often participate in archaeological digs themselves.

Best of all, collectors today find coins centuries old that are available and affordable. Although some of the rarest ancient coins have sold for thousands of dollars, many bronze specimens are within the reach of even the most modest budget. Many coin dealers carry good stocks of ancient coins. Other collectors are often willing to sell or trade their extra or duplicate ancients.

LYDIA—THE BIRTHPLACE OF COINS

There came a time in the seventh century B.C. when progressive thinkers realized that something was needed for trade, something durable, standard, portable, and easily recognized for its worth. They reasoned that if the weight, value, and consistency could be marked on an object in some way to assure its authenticity, it would soon replace other objects used in trade.

Most numismatic scholars believe that coins as we know them in the Western world were introduced about 640 or 630 B.C., in the kingdom of Lydia in ancient Asia Minor. These coins were crude lumps struck from electrum, a pale yellow combination of gold and silver that forms naturally when the two metals meld together. There was so much gold and silver in the soil that pellets of electrum tumbled down from the Lydian mountains to the river beds below.

We can imagine that a young and perhaps royal Lydian youth, hiking by a river, picked up a lump of electrum, flattened it between two rocks, and carried it home to his father as an interesting object. The idea that such an object had value and could be used for trade actually had a royal beginning; it is believed that coins were invented during the reign of King Ardys of Lydia.

It was necessary for the first electrum coins, called *staters* (STATE-ers), to be marked so that Lydians would recognize them as objects of value and a means of exchange. So the minters struck a lion on the front and punched a crude mark on the back. Just like our coins

Coins as we know them today were invented by the ancient Lydians. This Lydian coin, a half stater, is more than 2,500 years old.

today, staters had denominations. Standard weights gave them credibility as coins, and the Lydians learned to trust and use them.

The ancients soon learned to separate gold and silver and to weigh and stamp the metals in order to use them over and over. These pieces were not only durable, but also convenient for trade. They could even be used to measure wealth.

There is good reason to call a wealthy person "rich as Croesus." Croesus was a Lydian king (561–546 B.C.) who, according to legend, gave nearly four tons of gold as a tribute to the god of music and poetry, Apollo. Apollo, the legend continues, returned the favor by causing torrents of rain to keep Croesus from being burned alive by his enemies. Because of his high regard for the precious metal, Croesus decreed that the coins of his kingdom should be almost pure gold, instead of electrum. Gold coins soon drove electrum coins out of circulation.

Scholars differ over who first introduced round coins. One Chinese scholar claims that metal coins were used in China as early as the 20th century B.C. Others agree that the first coins should be credited to the Chinese, along with the invention of gunpowder, printing, and paper money. But more evidence is needed to support these claims. Most coin specialists believe that the invention of the round coins in China coincides with their first use in the West, during the seventh century B.C.

ANCIENT CHINESE COINS

The earliest round Chinese coins were distinctive. They had square holes in the center so they could be strung together. These strands of coins came to be known as *cash*, a familiar word to us today. One could carry around strings of cash to spend. We do know that cash coins were in use around the time of Confucius (551–479 B.C.), and were probably used to pay the workers who built the Great Wall in the third century A.D. These coins were used well into the twentieth century.

Some coin experts say that Oriental money is the most difficult to study because it is so complex. Among the many intricate marks on one Chinese coin is the imprint of a fingernail. Empress Wen Te marked her coinage by using her long nail to make a crescent-shaped indentation in the wax coin mold.

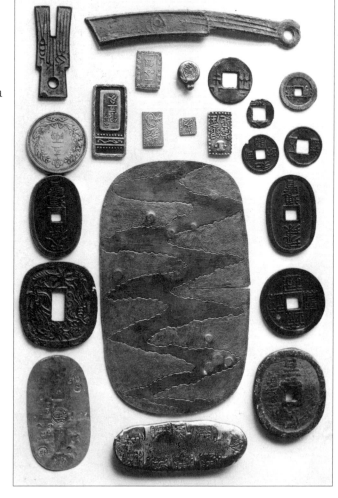

This collection of ancient gold and silver Japanese coins shows some of the beautiful designs used for Oriental coins.

GREEK AND ROMAN COINS

Coins have been collected almost from the time they were invented. The Romans appreciated the beauty of Greek coins; it is said the Emperor Augustus was a collector. Greek coin artists were masters at depicting their gods and goddesses with portrait coins. They designed coins portraying Zeus, the king of the gods; Athena, the goddess of wisdom, and Aphrodite, the goddess of love. The Romans paid tribute to their gods too, with coins depicting Jupiter, Venus, Mars, and others.

Because of coins we know the faces of many leaders and conquerors of the ancient world, such as Nero, Julius Caesar, Brutus, Augustus, Antony, and Cleopatra. (When they first see the coin of Cleopatra, many are often surprised at her appearance. Historians say Cleopatra's charm made up for her lack of beauty.)

Greek silver tetradrachm, c. 450 B.C. The obverse (top) shows Athena, the goddess of wisdom. The reverse (bottom) depicts an owl, also a symbol of wisdom.

This Macedonian coin (336–323 B.C.) was minted for Alexander the Great. The obverse (left) depicts the god Heracles (Hercules). The reverse (not shown) shows Heracles' father and king of the gods, Zeus.

Just as we honor our leaders on our coins today, the Romans honored their emperors with portrait coins. This Roman coin shows us how Julius Caesar looked.

Ancient coins carry the likenesses of real and mythical animals, birds (including the eagle, which appears on our coins today), fish, plants, fruits, and weaponry. Coins show us ancient ships, buildings, aqueducts, gates, and coliseums. They tell us of ancient politics and the structure of complex dynasties. Since there were no newspapers, coins often carried the political propaganda of the time. We can study art, styles of dress, hairdos, modes of transportation, and sports. Creative teachers of Latin, art, archaeology, architecture, and the classics often use ancient coins to bring their subjects to life.

Modern-day sports fans are not the first to have Olympic coins. The

Olympic games were first held in 776 B.C. One of the earliest known coins commemorating the ancient Olympic games is a Sicilian silver coin called a *tetradrachm* (TET-ra-dram), dated 480 B.C. It shows a *biga* (BIG-a), a two-horse chariot, with Nike, the goddess of victory, flying protectively overhead.

Two portraits of the king of the gods: Zeus (above) on a Greek silver tetradrachm (c. 336 B.C.) and Jupiter (below) on a Roman coin.

Roman coin depicting the infamous Emperor Nero (A.D. 37–68).

A noblewoman named Julia Maesa, who died about A.D. 225, is depicted on this Roman sestertius (se-STERSH-ee-us).

Above: Gold distater of Alexander the Great, 336–323 B.C. Below: Silver tetradrachm of Antiochus I, king of Syria, 280–261 B.C.

Silver shekel, A.D. 68–69. The obverse (left) shows a chalice, with the inscription "Shekel of Israel, year 3." The reverse shows a pomegranate plant, with the inscription "Jerusalem the Holy."

COINS FROM THE BIBLE

Some collectors specialize in biblical coins. Among the most familiar are the silver *denarius* issued by the Roman emperor Tiberius and the silver *shekel* of Tyre, which must have been among the 30 pieces of silver Judas received for the betrayal of Christ. The parable of the widow's mite refers to the lowly copper *lepton*.

Symbols of faith and hope adorned Jewish coins struck in Palestine from the Maccabean era to the time of Bar Kochba (39 B.C. to A.D. 135). An

example is silver and bronze coinage from the periods of the First and Second Revolt (A.D. 60–70 and 133–135), struck as the Jews tried to throw off the yoke of Rome.

The first coin to depict Christ was this gold solidus, minted for Emperor Justinian II (A.D. 669–711).

More than 1,900 years later, when the new state of Israel came into existence in 1948, the coin designers used symbols from the ancient series as a meaningful link to their ancient history. Collectors who wish to concentrate in this area can find excellent references on Jewish coinage and money in the Old and New Testaments.

THE MIDDLE AGES

As civilizations developed, coin designs became more elaborate and minters more skilled. In addition to gold and silver, other metals such as bronze, brass, copper, and silvered bronze were introduced for coins. Their use quickly spread throughout western civilization.

Our word "dollar" can be traced back to this coin, a Joachimsthaler, 1576, named for the German city in which it was struck, Joachimsthal. The name was eventually shortened to "taler," which later became "dollar."

The first person recorded in history as a specialist in the hobby and science of collecting coins was an early Renaissance man, Francesco Petrarcha (Petrarch), who lived from 1304 to 1374. An Italian poet and scholar devoted to the study of classics, Petrarcha left records telling of the pleasures of coin collecting.

Coins survived through fallen empires and the Dark Ages, remaining useful economic tools throughout the medieval and the Renaissance periods. Gutenberg and the miracle of printing made

An early Renaissance coin, the guildiner, minted in 1486 for Archduke Sigismund of Tyrol-Austria.

"Seventh bell" taler (1642), minted in Brunswick-Wolfenbuttel, Germany.

it possible to produce books on numismatics. Coins were a favorite subject for artists, who depicted them in rich paintings and engravings.

The origin of our word *dollar* can be traced back to this period in Europe. A heavy silver coin, *gulden groschen* (GUL-den GRO-shen), was struck in Tyrol in the late 15th century. The *Joachimsthaler* (yo-ACK-ims-tah-ler) was coined in the following century. Soon, the name for heavy, important silver coins was shortened to *thaler* (TAH-ler) or *taler*. When the United States was established, the colonists admired heavy silver coins. They vowed that the United States would have a heavy coin called a dollar. No one knows how or when the word *taler* became dollar.

Although coin collecting during this time was confined to kings, queens, popes, and, beginning in the 14th century, rich merchants, we are grateful to them for preserving beautiful specimens in their elaborate coin cabinets. Though many of these coins can be seen in museums, others have reached the numismatic marketplace.

Chapter 4

A HISTORY OF AMERICAN COINS

What culture shock it must have been for the earliest European settlers in North America. They had very little need for coins in an untamed environment. There certainly weren't any corner grocery stores. They had cut themselves off from Europe and its highly developed coinage system, except for the coins the colonists brought with them— probably more in sentiment than in expectation of trade at first. Their minds were on survival.

A 1964 Kennedy half dollar, one of America's most handsome coin designs.

American Indian wampum like this was also used as currency by early European settlers in North America.

These hardy people soon learned that they needed to trade with the native Indians in order to survive. At first the settlers bartered with the Indians. Soon they began to use the Indian's currency, *wampum*. Wampum was made of shells, usually clam or conch, with different values attached to white, black and purple shells. At times wampum was devalued as money when it was counterfeited. Later it was produced from other materials, mostly porcelain, for use by the Indians—even into this century.

The settlers also used their products as "coinage." In Virginia, tobacco was used; in Massachusetts, grain, fish, and furs. Bullets and gunpowder, so valuable to the colonists, could be used to pay for goods and services.

When European trading vessels began to arrive on the eastern shores, the settlers used the small supply of French, German, and English coins they had brought with them to pay for badly needed goods from the old countries.

There were some crude coins circulating in the New World. For instance, there was *hogge money* or *hoggies*, named for the wild-looking hog engraved on the coins. These coins were struck somewhere in Europe (historians aren't certain where) around 1616 for use in England's Sommer Islands (now Bermuda). There were also a few privately struck pieces in circulation. But the European traders wanted familiar coins for their goods.

As the colonists began to trade with the West Indies, bulky Spanish eight-reales, the "pieces of eight" of pirate fame, began to circulate in the colonies. To make small change, the coins were cut into sections called "two bits" (quarter of the coin) or "four bits" (half of the coin).

COLONIAL COINS

The proud, independent citizens of British America wanted their own coinage. John Hull of the Massachusetts Bay Colony was authorized to start a mint in 1652. It was here that the famous New England willow and pine tree shillings, named for their tree designs, were struck. Other colonies soon followed and began making their own coins and tokens, which are coin substitutes.

Early American coin designers often looked to the classics for legends (the inscriptions on a coin). For example, New Jersey coins made from 1786 to 1788 bore the Latin *E Pluribus Unum* ("One out of many"). This phrase, attributed to Vergil or Horace (both ancient Roman poets), symbolized the union of the colonies and the diverse origin of their people to these early coinmakers. It first appeared on U.S. coinage in 1795, on the reverse of the $5 gold piece as part of the Great Seal scroll

The pine tree shilling was one of the first colonial coin designs. All pine tree shillings are dated "1652," the year in which the first colonial mint was authorized, although minting did not begin until 1667.

The first coin issued by the United States was the Fugio cent, 1787.

(the ribbonlike band held in the eagle's beak). This is the official motto of the United States and appears on its coins to this very day. The 2¢ piece, minted from 1864 to 1873, was the first to carry the motto "In God We Trust." Congress decided in 1959 that the phrase would appear on all U.S. coins.

The early American minters often wanted to convey the message of liberty in their work. A good example is the 1787 Fugio cent, the first national coin authorized by Congress (but produced by private minters). On one side is a circular chain of 13 links (representing the 13 states) wrapped around the motto "We Are One." On the other side is a dial, hours of the day, the noon sun, and the Latin word *fugio* ("to flee"), signifying "time flies." Below the dial are the words "Mind Your Business." To the citizens of the new nation this meant work harder, not keep your affairs to yourself.

The Fugio cent is often called the Franklin cent because the legends of the coin have been attributed to Benjamin Franklin. Franklin had a great interest in the new nation's money, but he wanted to put a turkey, a bird native to America, on the coins instead of the classic eagle.

THE FIRST U.S. COINS

In 1791, after Congress adopted the Constitution and elected George Washington president, it authorized the first U.S. Mint in Philadelphia. The mint is believed to be the first public building in the new nation authorized by a congressional act. This shows how important having our own official money was to historic figures such as George Washington, Thomas Jefferson, Alexander Hamilton, and many others, including some of the signers of the Declaration of Independence.

The first four U.S. coins, dated 1792, were a silver-center cent, a birch cent, a half disme and a disme (that's right—disme, not dime). These coins are rare and have been sold at auctions for thousands of dollars.

Copper disme, 1792, predecessor of today's dime.

Reverse of white metal Birch cent, 1792, one of the first coins struck by the U.S. Mint. Named after engraver Robert Birch, who is believed to have designed the coin.

Flowing hair type silver dollar, 1794—the first U.S. dollar.

There was also a 1792 pattern quarter dollar, but only two of these coins are known to exist today. Legend has it that Martha Washington gave her precious tea service to supply the silver for these early coins, and she may have been the model for the female portrait on the coin. We have a painting showing Martha Washington inspecting the first coins, which reinforces these legends. The first regular U.S. coin issues, cents and half cents, were struck in 1793, beginning a series of magnificent gold, silver, and copper issues.

George and Martha Washington inspect the first coins at the U.S. Mint in a painting by John Ward Dunsmore.

The gold rush produced much gold, but very few coins. The frontier settlers, cut off from the U.S. Mint, started minting their own unofficial coins, which were used until 1864, when they were outlawed.

TERRITORIAL COINS

No true collector of U.S. coins ignores the private or territorial gold coins issued from 1830 to 1861, even though they are not recognized as official coins.

These coins are surrounded by the legends of the gold rush and the pioneers of the West. Pioneers moving out across the mountains and rivers found themselves faced with desperate need for coins in their new settlements. But they were very far away from the government's Philadelphia Mint. They had plenty of gold, but getting it to the mint to be processed and returned as coinage was next to impossible. So enterprising bankers, assayers, and private firms struck their own coins with their own denominations and designs to serve the demand.

The unofficial pieces were readily accepted by the people. They solved coin shortages in North Carolina, Colorado, Utah, and Oregon. They kept

Templeton Reid, a jeweler and gunsmith from Milledgeville, Georgia, struck these unofficial gold coins in 1830. Marked "ten dollars," these pieces are worth as much as $50,000 today because of their rarity.

During the Civil War, this cent was designed for the Confederacy by a Philadelphia engraver named Robert Lovett, Jr. Fearing arrest for aiding the enemy, Lovett never delivered the coins, but hid them in his basement instead.

up with the trade demands of California during its gold rush days, providing collectors with a colorful chapter in U.S. numismatic history. In 1864 the government declared the private and territorial coins illegal, conforming to the laws of the founding fathers that only the U.S. government could authorize coins.

WOMEN IN THE COIN WORLD

Martha Washington would no doubt be pleased at the present-day role of women in the coin world. Women have been appointed by U.S. presidents to occupy key government positions having to do with coins. For instance, there is U.S. treasurer Mary Ellen Withrow, appointed in 1994. You have probably seen her signature on paper money. The treasurer oversees operations at the Bureau of Engraving and Printing and the United States Mint.

The first woman mint director, Nellie Teyloe Ross, was interested in numismatics and welcomed advice from collectors. During her tenure as director (1933–53) a number of collectible commemorative coins were issued. In the 1960s and 1970s, mint directors Eva Adams and Mary Brooks were active supporters of numismatics. Adams opened the new Philadelphia Mint, and the Kennedy half dollar was produced during her administration. Brooks was responsible for the Bicentennial coins and for saving the old San Francisco Mint, a structure which had withstood the San Francisco earthquake, from demolition by turning it into a coin museum.

Donna Pope, who was appointed director of the mint in 1981, has achieved major breakthroughs in commemorative coin revival, new coin designs, the U.S. bullion coin program, and has instituted many technical advances in the mint.

In 1981, Elizabeth Jones was appointed the 11th chief sculptor and engraver of the United States, the first woman to hold the position. Under her direction some of the most artistic coin designs in modern history have been developed. These include her own work and that of the engraving staff located at the Philadelphia Mint.

The Smithsonian Institution's numismatic holdings, including the U.S. national coin collection, are in the hands of Elvira Clain-Stefanelli, executive director in charge of the national collection and an internationally known numismatic scholar.

Mary Ellen Withrow became treasurer of the United States in 1994. She is the twelfth woman to hold the post, and is one of the most qualified: she was treasurer of the state of Ohio before her Washington appointment. She directs the U.S. Mint and Bureau of Engraving and Printing.

Elvira Clain-Stefanelli, official keeper of the national coin collection at the Smithsonian Institution's Museum of American History, has a worldwide reputation as a prolific author, lecturer, and researcher. She is a member of the Citizen's Commemorative Coin advisory committee.

RECENT COLLECTIBLE COINS

The number of collectible coins has continued to grow in recent years, with more on the way.

A new era for collectors began in 1964 with the John F. Kennedy half dollar, struck to commemorate the assassinated president. Collectors also welcomed the Eisenhower dollar, the three handsome Bicentennial coins (a dollar, a half dollar, and a quarter), the Susan B. Anthony dollar, and commemorative issues for the 1984 Los Angeles Olympics, the Statue of Liberty, and the Bicentennial of the Constitution. The first U.S. gold and silver bullion coins, called "eagles," were issued to compete in the international bullion coin market.

In 1990 another Eisenhower dollar was issued, to commemorate the 100th anniversary of his birth. This coin was approved by President Reagan in 1988. Congress decided to honor its own Bicentennial with a coin in 1989. There may be many design changes on U.S. coins in the near future. Some lawmakers want to give a totally new look to U.S. coins. Fine arts advocates and collectors actively lobby for new portraits and designs for our coins.

Bullion coins are a convenient way for investors to buy, hold, and trade precious metals. U.S. bullion coins include the gold eagle (above) and the silver eagle (below).

THE KENNEDY HALF DOLLAR—MINIATURE MEMORIAL

On February 11, 1964, less than three months after John F. Kennedy was assassinated, a ceremony was held at the Philadelphia Mint to strike the first Kennedy half dollar.

An unprecedented hush fell over the Treasury officials, mint workers, and television and newspaper reporters crowded around a coining press to witness the first striking of coins in tribute to the fallen president.

Assistant Secretary of the Treasury Robert Wallace and Mint Director Eva Adams officiated the ceremony. A phone line to the Denver Mint was kept open, so that the first coins could be struck simultaneously in both locations.

At the Philadelphia Mint, the only sound was the heavy chugging of the coin press, which seemed extraordinarily loud on this solemn occasion. The first pristine half dollar with the profile portrait of the young President was removed from the coin press and carefully set aside. Two more coins were quickly struck. These coins were hand-delivered to the President's widow, Jacqueline Kennedy, and to the Kennedy children, Caroline and John, Jr.

By early March, the Philadelphia and Denver Mints had struck enough coins to begin circulation. The coins were immediately popular. It wasn't only coin collectors who put them aside: people treated the coins as miniature memorials, a feeling that spread around the world. There was great demand for the coins overseas.

How was the Kennedy half dollar produced in just a few short weeks? Usually it takes months to design and produce a new coin. And by U.S. law coin designs can be changed only every 25 years.

It was Mint Director Eva Adams, appointed by Kennedy in 1961, who coordinated every step of the process. Adams, a skilled attorney with a good knowledge of how things work on Capitol Hill, set a plan in motion.

Congress quickly approved the Kennedy half dollar; an act was passed on December 30, 1963, authorizing the minting of the coin. The new coin replaced the Franklin half dollar, first minted in 1948.

Fortunately, a handsome medallic portrait of President Kennedy already existed; it had been created by Chief Engraver Gilroy Roberts for a medal. When the design was shown to Jacqueline Kennedy, she approved it for the front of the coin.

Frank Gasparro of the U.S. Mint staff had designed the President's seal of office for another medal, and his design was adopted for the reverse of the coin.

Jacqueline Kennedy, Robert F. Kennedy, and Secretary of the Treasury Douglas Dillon were all consulted at various stages in the creation of the coin. Chief Engraver Roberts added the finishing touches to this handsome coin, whose beauty endures.

What will American coins of today say to collectors 2,000 years from now? Those who may study U.S. coins will see that Americans honored their presidential leaders just as the Romans did, with strong portraits. Coins will show that Americans cared about freedom, liberty, and justice. They will portray now a people worked, sacrificed, and fought to preserve its Constitution. Commemorative coins especially will tell a detailed story of how the nation grew. (Commemorative coins will be discussed further in Chapter 8.)

CHECKLIST

Coin collectors are a lot like sports fans—they like to keep records and statistics. They keep track of varieties, catalog sales, and record prices and performance. Compiling a checklist of the major U.S. coin types is good collector discipline. The list on the following pages will help you as you begin collecting. The amazing variety of coin designs explains the unusual descriptions some of the coins have. These are part of the unique language of coin collecting.

An ideal collection would contain one coin, in the best possible condition, of each type listed.

Major U.S. Coins by Type—Copper and Silver

Half Cents
1793, Flowing Hair
1794–1797, Liberty Cap
1800–1808, Draped Bust
1809–1836, Classic Head
1840–1857, Braided Hair

Large Cents
1793, Chain
1793, Wreath
1793–1796, Liberty Cup
1796–1807, Draped Bust
1808–1814, Classic Head
1816–1839, Coronet Head
1840–1857, Braided Hair

Small Cents
1856–1858, Flying Eagle
1859, Copper-Nickel
1860–1864, Indian Copper Nickel
1864–1909, Indian Bronze
1909–1958, Lincoln-Wheat Ears
1959 to date, Lincoln-Memorial

Two Cents
1864–1873, Two-Cent Piece

Three-Cent Nickel
1865–1889, Three-Cent Nickel

Three-Cent Silver
1851–1853, Variety 1
1854–1858, Variety 2
1859–1873, Variety 3

Five-Cent Nickel
1866–1867, Shield, Rays
1867–1883, Shield, No Rays
1883, Liberty Head, No Cents
1883–1913, Liberty Head with Cents
1913, Indian Head, Variety 1
1913–1938, Variety 2
1938 to date, Jefferson

Half Dimes
1794–1795, Flowing Hair
1796–1797, Draped Bust, Small Eagle
1800–1805, Draped Bust, Heraldic Eagle
1829–1837, Capped Bust
1837–1838, Seated Liberty, No Stars
1838–1859, Seated Liberty, Stars
1853–1855, Seated Liberty, Arrows
1860–1873, Seated Liberty, Legend

Dimes
1796–1797, Draped Bust, Small Eagle
1798–1807, Draped Bust, Heraldic Eagle
1809–1828, Capped Bust, Large
1828–1837, Capped Bust, Small
1837–1838, Seated Liberty, No Stars
1838–1860, Seated Liberty, Stars
1853–1855, Seated Liberty, Arrows
1860–1891, Seated Liberty, Legend
1873–1874, Seated Liberty, Arrows
1892–1916, Barber Type
1916–1945, Winged Liberty
1946 to date, Roosevelt

1815 Capped Bust half dollar.

1854 Seated Liberty half dollar.

Twenty-Cent Piece
1875–1878, Twenty-Cent Piece

Quarters
1796, Draped Bust, Small Eagle
1804–1807, Draped Bust, Heraldic
    Eagle
1815–1828, Capped Bust Large
1831–1838, Capped Bust Small
1838–1865, Seated Liberty, No Motto
1853, Seated Liberty, Arrows and Rays
1854–1855, Seated Liberty with Motto
1873–1874, Seated Liberty Arrows
1892–1916, Barber Type
1916–1917, Standing Liberty, Variety 1
1917–1930, Standing Liberty, Variety 2
1932 to date, Washington Type

Half Dollars
1794–1795, Flowing Hair

1796–1797, Draped Bust, Small Eagle
1801–1807, Draped Bust, Heraldic
    Eagle
1807–1836, Capped Bust, Lettered Edge
1836–1839, Capped Bust, Reeded Edge
1839–1866, Seated Liberty, No Motto
1853, Seated Liberty, Arrows and Rays
1854–1855, Seated Liberty, Arrows
1866–1891, Seated Liberty with Motto
1873–1874, Seated Liberty, Arrows
1892–1915, Barber Type
1916–1947, Walking Liberty
1948–1963, Franklin-Liberty Bell
1964 to date, Kennedy Type

Dollars
1794–1795, Flowing Hair
1795–1798, Draped Bust, Small Eagle
1798–1804, Draped Bust, Heraldic
    Eagle
1836–1839, Gobrecht
1840–1866, Seated Liberty, No Motto
1866–1873, Seated Liberty with Motto
1873–1885, U.S. Trade Dollar
1878–1921, Morgan Type
1921–1935, Peace Type
1971–1978, Eisenhower Type
1979–1982, Susan B. Anthony Type

Bicentennial reverses (the back of a coin) appear on the quarter, half dollar, and dollar with dual dating, 1776–1976. They were produced in 1975 and 1976.

MAJOR U.S. COINS BY TYPE—GOLD

Dollars
1849–1854, Liberty Head, Type 1
1854–1856, Indian Head, Type 2
1856–1889, Indian Head, Type 3

Quarter Eagles ($2.50)
1796, Capped Bust Right, No Stars
1796–1807, Capped Bust Right
1808, Capped Bust Left, Large
1821–1834, Capped Bust Left, Small
1834–1839, Classic Head
1840–1907, Liberty Coronet
1908–1929, Indian Head

Three Dollars
1854–1889, Indian Head

Four Dollars (Stella)
1879–1880, Flowing Hair

Half Eagles ($5.00)
1795–1798, Capped Bust, Small Eagle
1795–1807, Capped Bust Right,
    Heraldic Eagle
1807–1812, Capped Draped Bust
1813–1834, Capped Head

1834–1838, Classic Head
1839–1866, Liberty Coronet, No Motto
1866–1907, Liberty Coronet
1907–1908, Liberty Coronet
1908–1929, Indian Head

Eagles ($10.00)
1795–1797, Capped Bust, Small Eagle
1797–1804, Capped Bust Right,
    Heraldic Eagle
1838–1866, Liberty Coronet, No Motto
1866–1907, Liberty Coronet
1907–1908, Indian Head, No Motto
1908–1933, Indian Head

Double Eagles ($20.00)
1849–1866, Liberty Coronet, Without
    Motto on Reverse
1866–1876, Liberty, Twenty D.
1877–1907, Twenty Dollars
1907, Saint-Gaudens, Roman Numerals,
    High Relief
1907–1908, Saint-Gaudens, Arabic
    Numerals, No Motto
1908–1933, Saint-Gaudens

U.S. BULLION COINS

Silver Eagle
1986 to date, $1.00, Walking Liberty,
    Heraldic Eagle

Gold Eagles
1987 $25.00; 1988 to date, $5.00,
    $10.00, $25.00, $50.00

1929 Indian Head half eagle.

Chapter 5

STARTING YOUR COLLECTION

These silver coins were struck to commemorate the United Nations Decade for Women: Sudan (top), Turkey (bottom).

You don't need to be wealthy to start collecting coins.

Coin collecting is one of the most relaxing and most interesting hobbies, and it can be profitable as well. As a coin collector you will always have something of value to show for your efforts, beginning with the face value of the coins. How about starting with a set of U.S. coins from the year you were born? Suppose you were born in 1976, the year of the nation's Bicentennial celebration. You can put together an uncirculated set of your birthday coins for as little as $4.20. This would include a Bicentennial dollar, half dollar, and quarter with dual dates (1776 and 1976) and a dime, nickel, and cent dated 1976.

You could obtain a Bicentennial year set in several ways. First, check the coins you may have in your pocket or around the house. Bicentennial coins are still in circulation, but they are becoming more scarce. So are the 1976 dimes, nickels, and cents. And because these coins have been in circulation they may not be in the condition you want for your collection.

The next step is to tell your family and friends that you are collecting coins. You'll be surprised at the variety of coins people have around their homes. People are often willing to share these coins because they are interested in learning more about them. You may find coins that have been in your family for years.

If there is a coin club in your area, by all means join. You will be warmly welcomed. You will find opportunities to trade with or buy from fellow collectors, who will help you along with advice as well as coins. For information about coin clubs in your area, ask a local coin dealer or write to the American Numismatic Association, 818 North Cascade Avenue, Colorado Springs, Colorado 80903–3279.

It's also a good idea to write to the United States Mint to get your name and address on its mailing list, which contains millions of other collectors. You will receive notices of how and when to buy new U.S. coins directly from the mint. (For the address of the U.S. Mint, see p. 105.)

GUIDEBOOKS

When you start collecting coins, it's like traveling down a new and exciting road with many turns. It makes good sense to have a map. Get yourself a coin guidebook.

Many guidebooks are like numismatic encyclopedias. They are filled with historic information about official and unofficial coins, and with illustrations, mintages, and prices. There are guidebooks just for beginning collectors. Guidebooks are available at libraries, bookstores, magazine stands, and coin shops. Some coin clubs order new guidebooks for their members each year so that they will have up-to-date information and basic coin prices.

The moment you open a guidebook you will see a new language—mint marks, type sets, obverse, proof, alloy, grade. The glossary at the end of this book will help you to understand these terms.

AN ESSENTIAL TOOL

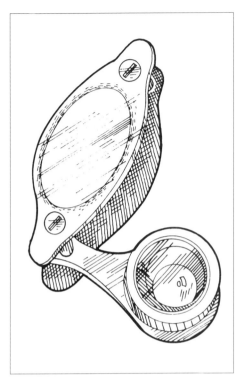

A magnifying glass will let you see the important details that separate an ordinary coin from a valuable find.

One of the good things about coin collecting is that very little is needed in the way of tools.

The most important tool a collector can own is a magnifying glass. A good collector is never without one. Shop carefully for your glass and get the strongest one you can afford. The magnifying power (3X, 5X, etc.) should be marked on the glass. Advanced collectors prefer *loupes*, the small, folding magnifiers used by jewelers. You may wish to start with one of these.

Once you get a magnifying glass, begin to examine your coins closely. Take a look at a 1996 Lincoln cent. Check the details of Lincoln's hair, beard, and cheekbones. These are the points where the coin will wear, affecting its condition and value. Look at the Lincoln Memorial on the reverse (back) of the coin. Do you see the statue of Lincoln? Did you know it was on the coin? Most people don't.

Now see if you can find an Indian Head type cent. These were last struck in 1909, but they are not too hard to find. Ask around—many people have them. They are not too expensive if you must buy one. Take a look at the portrait on the obverse (front) of the coin. You will be studying an Indian princess and the feathers and bonnet ribbon on her headdress. On the reverse you will find laurel leaves.

With a magnifying glass you will really be able to see your coins. You can study the details of the many different coin designs. You can also check the condition of your coins, see whether they are worn or nicked and scratched. This will be important when you begin to learn about grading coins.

GRADES AND RARITY

Grade is the standard by which the condition of a coin is judged. The better a coin's condition, the better its grade will be and the greater its value.

There are different systems for grading coins. Descriptions such as "brilliant uncirculated" or "very fine" are used by some dealers. Others use a numerical grading system, sometimes called the "shorthand" method of grading.

The American Numismatic Association has developed a 15-point system for determining coin conditions, ranging from proof (the most perfect coin) to AG-3 (about good), a coin in poor condition, very worn, almost smooth.

There are three professional firms who will grade coins for a fee, but it's best for a new collector to learn how to grade. You can start by asking a dealer or a fellow collector to help. There are books on grading available, and some collector organizations offer grading seminars, where you can learn from experts.

The number of coins produced is also important. Some coins are scarcer than others. Rarity as well as grade determines coin values. These factors are important as you build your collection, especially if you decide to sell the coins one day and start another series.

Your first priority, however, should be to start collecting the best coins that you can afford, even if they are worn. Part of the fun and challenge of collecting is to be constantly on the lookout for chances to upgrade your collection by replacing worn coins with ones in better condition. There will be plenty of time to accomplish this.

CHOOSING YOUR COLLECTION

Once you have browsed through a guidebook enough to get a sense of the scope of coin collecting, you will want to choose a goal for your collection. Don't worry about your choice; just jump in. Veteran collectors may put together many different collections in a lifetime, finishing one with much

A 1987 British proof set. A proof set contains one of each type of coin produced during the year, in near-perfect condition.

satisfaction only to start another. Everyone starts somewhere.

You may decide to assemble a 20th-century U.S. type set. For this you will need cents, nickels, dimes, quarters, half dollars, and dollars of each design produced by the United States Mint, beginning in 1900. Don't worry about gold coins or rarities at this point. These cost too much for a young collector. (Here your family may help at birthdays and holidays with gifts of coins too expensive for an allowance.)

Or you may wish to specialize in one series of coins. A series is all of the coins of a particular denomination, design, and type. Some series are easier to complete than others, because some coins are more scarce and therefore more expensive. For example, it is easier to assemble a series of Roosevelt dimes than a series of Lincoln cents.

Did you say "penny"? One of the first lessons a collector of U.S. coins learns is that there is no penny in official U.S. coinage. The term "penny" is exclusive to the British coinage system, not ours. Use the word "cent" and you are immediately identified as a well-informed collector. (People have proposed that we do away with the little cent, but a recent national poll showed that it is still popular.)

WHERE TO SHOP

Coin dealers are a prime source of coins—after all, it's their business. They maintain their stock by buying and selling coins. Like all businessmen, dealers need to make a profit from the coins they sell, so don't expect to buy coins at face value. But most dealers are willing to work with new collectors. After all, they want you to be their customer. Dealers have been known to reduce the price of a first coin in order to encourage a new collector.

If you have an opportunity to attend a coin show, be sure to go. You will never forget your first experience at a coin show where there are tables and cases of coins offered for sale. Coin magazines and newspapers will alert you to when and where coin shows are held. Also watch your local newspaper for events in your area.

If you live too far away from either a coin club or a coin shop, you can have fun buying, trading and even selling by mail. Weekly coin newspapers are filled with news and feature stories about coins, as well as up-to-the-minute price trends. They also provide a marketplace for dealers and collectors. There are pages of advertisements for many kinds of coins at prices to fit every budget.

The largest coin dealers in the world, as well as collectors who want to sell a few duplicates, use coin newspapers to reach collectors. There is built-in protection for mail-order transactions—most coin publications are very careful about their advertisers. Also, collector and dealer organizations have strict codes of ethics so that buyers and sellers may deal with each other with confidence.

The 1937 Edward VIII pattern crown was designed, but never circulated—England's King Edward VIII gave up the throne to marry the woman he loved.

Monthly coin magazines offer the same opportunities with a bit more time for "armchair" coin shopping and for learning from their in-depth feature stories. These magazines find their way into numismatic libraries as sources for research. If you go to such a library, you might find it interesting to look at coin magazines from the last century for a historical view of how collecting has developed.

COINS FROM AROUND THE WORLD

Some of the most interesting coins are produced in other parts of the world and are readily available, many at well under a dollar. Guidebooks are not just for U.S. coins. Giant guidebooks resembling metropolitan telephone directories include listings of coins from dozens of countries. You can assemble collections of coins depicting animals, flowers, and birds. You can even assemble a set of coins from around the world dedicated to peace.

Coins can be ordered directly from some mints abroad or from sources in this country for import coins. (For a list of major mints around the world, see pp. 105–107.) Coins from Canada and Mexico are beautiful and easily obtained. World coin collectors who order from overseas say there is an added bonus—there is something exciting about opening a package carrying colorful stamps and seals from distant places. The fastest way to buy world coins, though, is to find them in your own country. Check the ads in coin newspapers, magazines, and dealer price lists. Coin auctions and shows present many opportunities to buy coins from around the world.

If you discover that world coins are your primary interest, you may want to join a coin club devoted to this specialization.

Books are important tools for collectors. This is one collector's numismatic library.

Chapter 6

CARING FOR COINS

One of the first lessons a coin collector learns is how to handle a coin.

Always hold a coin, no matter what its condition, by placing two fingers on the rim. This way you can turn it in your hand and study it without damaging the coin's surfaces. This carefulness will mark you as a true collector who knows that finger marks and the reaction of the chemistry of your own fingertips with the metal of a coin can damage a coin.

To avoid damaging the surface of a coin, hold it by the rim.

Collectors are always on guard to protect their coins against nicks and scratches. True, such abuses appear on some old coins and even serve to identify certain rare coins, but you should take every precaution to protect the condition of your coins. Never throw coins together in a box where they can bump or dent each other. Dropping a rare coin can drastically diminish its value.

STORING YOUR COLLECTION

Fortunately for collectors, modern chemistry has introduced better ways to house coins. The better the condition of a collection, the more specialized its protection becomes. Collectors know they must guard against such enemies as sulfur, acids, foam rubber, oily substances, and polyvinyl chloride (PVC).

PVC is a chemical that was used to process the plastic in earlier coin holders. After a time collectors discovered that the chemical was interacting with the metal in the coin to create an oozy substance on the coin's surface. These holders are still on the market, but collectors should have no trouble identifying them. They are more pliable than the safer polyethylene holders and they have a greasy, sticky feel to them. Holders with PVC may also have a rainbow look to them when held up to a light.

Convenient, inexpensive coin folders and albums are available to collectors. Manufactured from heavy cardboard, these albums help collectors organize the most popular coins by date and mint. Cardboard folders and albums helped to popularize the hobby of coin collecting when they were introduced in the 1930s. You can readily find them in coin shops, bookstores, and hobby centers. These albums and folders are fine for inexpensive coins.

As you upgrade your collection you'll want to improve the housing of your more valuable coins. The paper from cardboard storage materials can "dust" the coins. It also can tarnish coins as the metal reacts with the paper.

Some albums use slides made from inert plastic, which does not react with metal. These are safe and allow you to see both sides of

"Slabs," or encapsulated holders, are a recent innovation. The sealed plastic holder protects the coin against wear and displays the year, grade, and other information.

each coin. Some collectors prefer to store their coins in inert Plexiglas acrylic plastic holders, which are available for nearly every coin series. Attractive, transportable displays can be created by using these holders. These holders can even be custom-made for your collection.

The newest method of housing coins is encapsulation, using a holder commonly called a *slab*. First developed by a commercial coin grading service, an enterprise formed by a group of coin dealers, the slab encapsulates a coin in a plastic holder, along with the date, denomination, grade, and other relevant information. The slab quickly became familiar to dealers and collectors as a new way to buy and sell coins. Slabs are used everywhere now—at shops, in coin shows, and in mail-order purchases.

The American Numismatic Association also uses encapsulated holders to protect many coins in its museum. It offers an authentication service for a fee to collectors and conducts grading seminars, but no longer grades coins for a fee. Collectors can use the services of grading professionals.

If you are lucky enough to inherit coins, check them for that archenemy, PVC. Be sure to transfer your coins into proper housing. Even some small transparent envelopes, safe as they seem, invite PVC contamination. Some products can remove PVC from coins, but this requires care and skill. It's best to get expert advice and assistance before you try it.

CLEANING COINS

Forget about cleaning a coin, no matter how tempting it may be to use soap or scouring powder in an effort to restore its luster. Not only are you damaging the coin, but you are also diminishing its value.

If you pick up a coin from the ground and need to remove the dirt in order to identify it, you would be forgiven for this kind of surface cleaning. Gently wipe a coin with a soft cloth to remove the surface dirt. Never polish or rub a coin. Certain kinds of coin cleaning, if done by an expert, are recognized by some collectors as necessary; for example, in the case of encrusted coins recovered from the deep sea by treasure hunters.

Use of commercial coin cleaners requires expertise. Experienced collectors will warn you that cleaning coins is risky, so when in doubt, don't clean a coin.

Chapter 7

HOW COINS ARE MADE

Early coins were literally struck. It took a hammer with some strength behind it to produce ancient and medieval coins. (Sometimes collectors call this method of minting coins the "armstrong" method.)

A punch and an anvil were used to create the first crude coin designs. A mighty blow of the hammer on a blank, a piece of metal, stamped one coin at a time. Each coin was slightly different because there was no way to accurately control its shape or thickness.

At first the dies (the metal punches that carry the design) had a raised surface so that the finished coin would have a deep or concave design hammered into it. Later

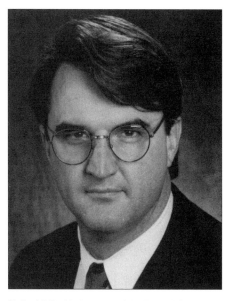

Phillip N. Diehl, director of the United States Mint, is first director in history to operate the mint on its own revenues. In 1995 Congress authorized the biggest change in the mint's 200-year history. The Mint no longer must depend on annual government appropriations for its billion-dollar enterprise. A $30 million upgrade of plant and equipment promises higher-quality coins at lower cost.

engravers reversed the dies so that the designs on the coin would be raised like those of our coins today. These dies are called *incuse* (in-KYOOS) or *intaglio* (in-TAL-ee-o).

Because each one is slightly different, ancient coins present modern collectors with a variety of interesting specimens for study. We appreciate the enterprise of the first coiners and admire the artistry of the die engravers, even though the coins they produced are not perfect. These engravers gave us, for example, the beautiful Greek coins so representative of their art and culture.

The ancients also produced coins by casting. To cast pieces they heated bronze until it melted and poured it into molds with designs at the bottom. After a cooling process, coins emerged. Romans used designs of birds, animals, and grain on their cast coins. Casting, however, was a slow process, too awkward and inefficient for the Romans. They were people on the move! They wanted more and more coins to carry on trade.

ROMAN COINMAKING

The Romans invented hinged dies so that coins could be aligned when a heated coin blank was placed between the top and bottom dies to receive designs.

The art of minting, first performed by traveling craftsmen, was soon centralized in hot, busy mints, with all the operations under one roof. As more mints were established, there were more trained minting specialists, understudies, and workers (often slaves).

Even then there were counterfeiters—culprits who shaved or clipped the edges from coins to get the precious metal to make coins for themselves. To defeat counterfeiters, Greek and Roman coin designers introduced coins with serrated or notched edges and beading. If these marks were disturbed it meant that someone had tampered with the coin.

One of the best records we have of ancient coinmaking was discovered during the excavation of Pompeii, a city buried for centuries in volcanic ash from the eruption of Mount Vesuvius in A.D. 79. Archaeologists found a fresco (wall mural) in Vetti House, a mansion built a few years before the volcanic destruction, depicting cherubs minting. The fresco gives us an overview of the ancient minting process.

Collectors in the U.S. can see a modern-day interpretation of the fresco at the Philadelphia Mint. Seven Favrile glass mosaics were created at the turn of the century under the direction of Louis C. Tiffany for the third Philadelphia mint. These national treasures were moved piece by piece to the present mint.

As the Roman Empire declined (after A.D. 476), coinage and minting seems to have become suspended in time, with little improvement; the same old processes were used, with hammers striking in cluttered rooms. Here again artists tell us the story: woodcuts and engravings of the period show minters using the primitive hammer-and-anvil techniques.

THE RENAISSANCE

It wasn't until the Renaissance that engraving processes and coin designs began to improve. Leonardo da Vinci, the Florentine painter, sculptor, and engineer, studied and planned improvements in the coining process.

Counterfeiting became more of a problem than ever during the Renaissance. It became so serious in England that counterfeiters were executed by the cruelest methods of the day.

Late in the 15th century coining entered the machine age with the invention of the screw (or mill) press. The screw press used pressure to

This 18th-century engraving from Diderot's Encyclopedia shows a hand-operated screw press.

squeeze the coin design onto the blank. It took two people to lower and raise the mechanism containing the die. They swung giant arms back and forth in rhythm while a third person set a coin blank under the die and removed it once it was stamped. This was risky business for the coin setter—bad timing could lead to serious injury.

European minters welcomed the screw press as the first coin production breakthrough in centuries. The hammer-and-anvil method soon disappeared, but even to this day we say that we "strike" coins.

Hand-operated screw presses continued to be used well into the 18th century. Denis Diderot, a French publisher, included a series of engravings in his 1715 encyclopedia that furnish us with an accurate description of the 18th-century coin press process.

quadruple dies, to experimental presses that stamp out coins like cookies, and presses capable of striking as many as 800 coins per minute. Single strokes, however, produce quality coinage and allow for longer die life.

U.S. coins are currently manufactured at mints in Philadelphia, Denver, San Francisco, and West Point. The technical staff of the U.S. Mint constantly monitors coin production at each facility from its headquarters in Washington, D.C.

Modern mints are efficient factories, yet there is still an age-old mystique associated with the production of money that sets them apart from other industrial shops.

Using the latest equipment, the U.S. Mint produces nearly 20 billion coins each year. Here, a metal strip called a clad is fed into a punching machine (above), which punches out round coin blanks (right).

Blanks are fed into the coin press, where dies impress the design. Here, a quarter has just been struck.

Coin dies contain the design of the coin in reverse.

If you live near a mint, plan to pay it a visit. All of the mints have regular visiting hours. (Be sure to check the hours ahead of time.) Shops at the mints sell collector coins and books. Mint tours are among the nation's top attractions for visitors and for student field trips.

PROOF AND UNCIRCULATED COINS

Proof coins, produced just for collectors, are minted, handled, and packaged differently from circulating coinage. They are struck twice with specially prepared dies on polished planchets (the disk on which the dies are impressed). Proof coins are handled like fine jewels at every step of the way in order to produce the finest coin possible. When they are completed, they are packaged in special holders to preserve their quality.

Uncirculated coins, also called "business strikes," are coins that have never been released for use in the economy. Uncirculated coins are minted the same way as circulated coins, but they appeal to collectors because they show none of the signs of wear found on circulated coins.

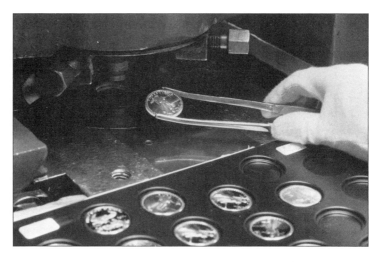

Proof coins are the highest-quality coins, and they are handled with care at every step of the minting process. A mint operator (above) removes a newly struck proof gold Eagle from the press.

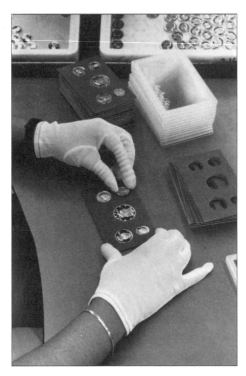

A proof set being assembled (left). The U.S. Mint packages these sets especially for collectors.

A white-gloved mint operator (right) places an encapsulated gold Eagle into a velvet case.

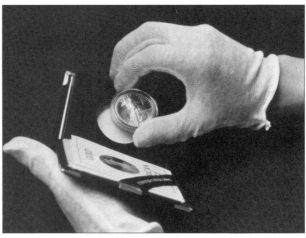

The U.S. Mint offers proof and uncirculated sets to hobbyists each year. Uncirculated sets are often called mint sets.

Most major mints in the world have proof and uncirculated coins available. A good place to see collector coins from around the world is at a coin show. Mints will often have display and sales areas at major conventions.

MINT MARKS

You can find out where a U.S. coin was minted by reading its mint mark.

Mint marks have helped officials from ancient times to locate the source of a coin if, for example, minting problems develop. Today we call this quality control. Collectors like to know where a coin is minted, too. Some mints did not produce as many coins in certain years. A study of mintage figures by individual mints tells the collector that these coins are scarcer than others—and thus worth more.

Here are the mint marks of U.S. coins:

C—Charlotte Mint, North Carolina
CC—Carson City Mint, Nevada
D—Dahlonega Mint, Georgia
D—Denver Mint, Colorado
O—New Orleans Mint, Louisiana
P—Philadelphia Mint, Pennsylvania
S—San Francisco Mint, California
W—West Point Mint, New York

Four of these mints are operating today: Denver, Philadelphia, San Francisco, and West Point.

The Philadelphia mint mark is the oldest, and the West Point mint mark is the newest. West Point was a bullion depository before it began to mint coins. It produced so many coins that it was given its own mint mark in 1984.

Mint marks are usually found on the reverse (back) of older coins. The Charlotte mark is found only on gold coins, and the Dahlonega gold coins from 1838 to 1861 carry the D marks. The three-cent silver coin of 1851 was struck in New Orleans and carries the O mint mark.

After 1967 the location of the mint mark was standardized so that the mark would appear on the obverse (front) of all U.S. coins. The Lincoln cent already carried the mint mark on the obverse.

Look for the S mint mark on 1908 and 1909 Indian cents under the wreath on the reverse of the coins. Liberty nickels struck in 1912 at the

San Francisco and Denver Mints are marked on the reverse, left of the word CENTS.

Finding the mark on a Buffalo nickel is simple—it's always on the back of the coin under the words FIVE CENTS. Not so with Jefferson nickels. At first the mark was placed at the right of the building on the back. From 1942 to 1945 the mark appeared above the Jefferson monument dome on the back of the coin. Then in 1968 it was moved to the obverse between the date and Jefferson's shoulder.

The marks on half dimes are found either within or below the wreath on the back. The same is true for older dimes. Beginning with the Mercury type (1916–1945), the mark is found on the reverse just to the left of the fasces (bundle of rods). Beginning in 1946 the mark appears to the left of the base of the torch. Since 1968 the mark has been placed on the obverse, above the date.

Twenty-cent pieces and quarters of the older variety show mint marks under the eagle on the back. After 1916 the mint marks on quarters were moved to the left of the date on the front. Washington quarters minted from 1932 to 1964 are marked under the eagle on the back. In 1968 the mark was moved to the right of the hair ribbon on the front.

Since 1968 the mint marks on the Kennedy half dollars have been above the date. They were moved from the 1964 location, to the left of the olive branch. Franklin halves (1948–1963) show the mark above the Liberty Bell. The 1838 and 1839 O (for New Orleans) half dollars show the mint mark over the date. Until 1915 the marks on all half dollars are on the reverse under the eagle. From 1917 the marks show on the lower left of the reverse.

Old type dollars carry their mint marks on the reverse, under the eagle. The mark moved near the eagle's wing when the Peace dollars were struck (1921–1935). The Anthony dollar shows the mark near Susan B. Anthony's shoulder, on the left.

Some coins may have no mint mark at all. For instance, if you are looking at U.S. coins struck at the Philadelphia Mint before 1979, you won't find a mint mark. It was taken for granted that unmarked coins were the product of the "mother mint." An exception is nickels struck at the

The U.S. Mint in Philadelphia is one of four facilities that produce U.S. coins. The others are in Denver, San Francisco, and West Point.

Philadelphia Mint from 1942 to 1945, which carry a P mark because the alloy was changed from nickel to a "wartime alloy" of copper, silver, and manganese; nickel was needed for the war effort.

THE ART OF THE COIN

Public interest in the art of the coin is growing. This is partly because of new coins that reflect a variety of artistic approaches. Chief Engraver Elizabeth Jones is known for her classical approach, reflected in coins like the 1982 Washington commemorative, which depicts George Washington on a horse. The heraldic eagle reverse on the $1 Silver Eagle, designed by engraver John Mercanti, is another recent artistic coin.

Some of the beautiful U.S. coin designs have resulted from national design competitions. The 1938 Jefferson nickel and the 1976 Bicentennial dollar, half dollar, and quarter are examples. All four of these coins were created by designers who won competitions. Many of the competitions are

Felix Schlag, designer of the Jefferson nickel.

by invitation only, but the competition for the Bicentennial coins was open to anyone, and submissions were received from kindergarten students as well as accomplished professional artists. The winners were chosen by a panel of selected artists.

Designers are being given more recognition for their work. For a designer to have his or her initials appear on a coin is a mark of numismatic distinction. Felix Schlag, whose design won the competition for the 1938 Jefferson nickel, received a $1,000 prize for his efforts. But 28 years later he received a much more important prize. In 1966 Mint Director Eva Adams presented Schlag with the first Jefferson nickel to carry the designer's initials. His initials appear on every nickel struck since then, a lasting tribute to the artist who created them.

Sometimes famous artists have been hired to design coins. In 1905 President Theodore Roosevelt invited the Irish-born American sculptor Augustus Saint-Gaudens to design a new gold coin.

Most of the credit for beautiful U.S. coins is due to the talents of the U.S. Mint's staff of engravers. They produce their own coin designs and refine the designs received from the mint's coining processes.

At age 22 engraver Dennis Williams won a Bicentennial design competition. His design appears on the reverse of the Eisenhower dollar.

THE MOST BEAUTIFUL U.S. COIN

President Theodore Roosevelt was famous for leading his Rough Riders in a charge up a San Juan hill during the Spanish-American War. Coin collectors appreciate him for a different kind of battle. He fought for better coin designs. He was responsible for what is considered the most beautiful U.S. coin, the Saint-Gaudens type $20 gold piece, minted from 1907 to 1933.

Roosevelt wanted U.S. coins to have a classical look, and he led the campaign for new designs with characteristic vigor.

In 1905 the famous sculptor Augustus Saint-Gaudens had delighted

President Roosevelt with a design for his inaugural medal. A year later the president asked Saint-Gaudens to design a coin.

"My dear Saint-Gaudens," Roosevelt wrote on November 6, 1905, "how is the gold coinage design coming along? I want to make a suggestion. It seems to me worth while to try for a really good coinage, though I suppose there will be a revolt about it. I was looking at some gold coins of Alexander the Great today, and I was struck by their high relief. Would not it be well to have our coins in high relief, and also to have the rims raised?"

Theodore Roosevelt led the Rough Riders during the Spanish-American War.
As president, he also led a vigorous campaign for new artistic U.S. coin designs.

Sculptor Augustus Saint-Gaudens at work in his studio.

The first designs from Saint-Gaudens pleased President Roosevelt, who called them "simply splendid." However, when the first coins were struck, mint officials found that the design was not compatible with their equipment, and the lovely designs would soon wear down once they were circulated. And bankers complained that the coins wouldn't stack.

So the height of the design was lowered, and the first extremely high-relief and high-relief strikes were labeled trial or experimental pieces. The lower-design Saint-Gaudens type $20 gold coin continued to circulate until 1933.

The U.S. Mint revived but modified the Saint-Gaudens design in 1986 for its American Eagle $20 gold bullion coin: Secretary of the Treasury James A. Baker ordered that the artistic Saint-Gaudens image of Liberty be slimmed down, much to the dismay of Saint-Gaudens devotees, including many in the numismatic community.

Chapter 8

COMMEMORATIVE COINS

Queen Isabella of Spain appears on this coin commemorating the Columbian Exposition of 1893.

Commemorative coins are produced to honor important people, places, and historic events. Commemoratives help us to preserve and celebrate our history.

The tradition of commemorative coins goes back to ancient times. The Greeks and Romans produced handsome commemoratives to celebrate victories in battle. An Athenian decadrachm, dating from 467 B.C., was struck to celebrate the defeat of the Persians by Athens. Another decadrachm, struck later in the fifth century B.C., is believed to have been minted in Syracuse to celebrate the defeat of an Athenian expedition to Sicily in 413 B.C.

Commemorative coins celebrate historic people and events. This $5 gold piece with a modernistic eagle design commemorates the Bicentennial of the Constitution in 1987.

Battle of Gettysburg commemorative half dollar. The obverse (above) pictures Generals Lee and Grant.

The U.S. Mint has been producing beautiful gold and silver commemoratives since 1892. U.S. commemorative coins have depicted covered wagons, beavers, and bears. They have honored great people such as Daniel Boone, Booker T. Washington, and many others, from Pilgrims to presidents.

The first woman to appear on a U.S. coin is on one of the early commemoratives. Oddly enough, she is not an American, but Queen Isabella of Spain, who appears on the Columbian Exposition commemorative issued in 1893. The most recent woman to be depicted on a U.S. coin is Eunice Kennedy Shriver, on a 1995 Special Olympics World Games dollar.

There was a time when the U.S. Mint stopped producing commemorative coins. In 1954 there was concern about a possible shortage of coins. The economy was expanding rapidly, and the mint could barely keep up with the tremendous demand for new coins. Congress decided to stop authorizing new commemoratives so that the mint could use all of its resources to produce coins for everyday use.

In 1982 a new era in U.S. commemorative coins began when Congress authorized a silver half dollar to celebrate George Washington's 250th birthday, the first new commemorative in 28 years. This coin proved so successful that a year later Congress approved gold and silver commemorative coins to honor the 1984 Los Angeles Olympics. Sales of the Olympic commemoratives raised $74 million to help finance the Los Angeles games.

In quick succession, in 1986 and 1987, the U.S. Mint was directed to produce two more artistic and historic gold coins to commemorate the centennial of the Statue of Liberty and the bicentennial of the U.S. Constitution. The Statue of Liberty coin raised more than $83 million to restore the statue and to benefit the Statue of Liberty/Ellis Island Foundation. Profits from the Constitution coins went to the general fund of the federal treasury.

Commemorative coins are as popular as ever with collectors and the public. Congress is receptive to introducing new commemoratives, since the programs not only pay for themselves, but also make money for the government. No program expenses are paid with taxpayer dollars.

If you wish to collect the U.S. commemorative series, you'll find dealers who specialize in stocks of these coins in every condition, including those for a beginner's budget. As you assemble your collection, you'll find plenty of opportunities to upgrade your coins and to add new types, varieties, and mint marks.

Silver half-eagle commemorating the centennial of the Statue of Liberty in 1986.

United States coins in gold, silver, and clad metals, commemorating the Atlanta Centennial Olympic games, are filled with action and symbolism. Top, 1996 Olympic commemorative gold five dollar coin; center, 1996 silver dollar; bottom, 1996 half dollar. (Designs shown are not actual coins.)

U.S. COMMEMORATIVE COINS, 1892–1996

Silver

Columbian Exposition, 1892–1893
Isabella quarter, 1893
Lafayette dollar, 1900
Panama Pacific Exposition, 1915
Illinois Centennial, 1918
Maine Centennial, 1920
Pilgrim Tercentenary, 1920–1921
Missouri Centennial, 1921
Alabama Centennial, 1921
Grant Memorial, 1922
Monroe Doctrine Centennial, 1923
Huguenot Walloon Tercentenary, 1924
Lexington Concord Sesquicentennial, 1925
Stone Mountain Memorial, 1925
California Diamond Jubilee, 1925
Fort Vancouver Centennial, 1925
Sesquicentennial of American Independence, 1926
Oregon Trail Memorial, 1926, 1928, 1933–1934, 1936–1939
Vermont Sesquicentennial (Bennington), 1927
Hawaiian Sesquicentennial, 1928
Maryland Tercentenary, 1934
Texas Centennial, 1934–1938
Daniel Boone Bicentennial, 1934–1938
Connecticut Tercentenary, 1935
Arkansas Centennial, 1935–1939
Hudson, New York, Sesquicentennial, 1935
San Diego-Pacific Exposition, 1935–1936
Old Spanish Trail, 1935
Rhode Island Tercentenary, 1936
Cleveland Great Lakes Exposition, 1936
Wisconsin Centennial, 1936
Cincinnati Musical Center, 1936
Long Island Tercentenary, 1936
York County, Maine, Centennial, 1936

Bridgeport, Connecticut, Centennial, 1936
Lynchburg, Virginia, Sesquicentennial, 1936
Elgin, Illinois, Centennial, 1936
Albany, New York, 1936
San Francisco-Oakland Bay Bridge, 1936
Columbia, South Carolina, Sesquicentennial, 1936
Delaware Tercentenary, 1936
Battle of Gettysburg, 1936
Norfolk, Virginia, Bicentennial, 1936
Roanoke Island, North Carolina, 1937
Battle of Antietam, 1937
New Rochelle, New York, 1938
Iowa Centennial, 1946
Booker T. Washington, 1946–1951
Booker T. Washington-George Washington Carver, 1951–1954
George Washington, 1982
Los Angeles Olympics, 1983–1984
Statue of Liberty, 1986
Constitution Bicentennial, 1987
Olympics, 1988
Congress, 1989
Eisenhower, 1990
Mount Rushmore, 1991
Korean War, 1991
USO, 1991
Olympic, 1992
White House, 1992
Columbus, 1992
Madison/Bill of Rights, 1993
Jefferson, 1993
World Cup Soccer, 1994
Prisoner of War, 1994
Vietnam Veterans, 1994
Women in Military, 1994
U.S. Capitol, 1994
Civil War, 1995
Shriver, 1995

Olympic Gymnastics, 1995
Olympic Blind Runner, 1995
Olympic Cycling, 1995
Olympic Field and Track, 1995

Gold
Louisiana Purchase dollar, 1903
Lewis and Clark Exposition dollar,
    1904–1905
Panama Pacific Exposition $1, $2.50,
    $50, 1915
McKinley Memorial dollar, 1916–1917
Grant Memorial dollar, 1922
U.S. Sesquicentennial $2.50, 1926
Olympic eagle, 1984
Statue of Liberty half-eagle, 1986
Constitution eagle, 1987
Olympic eagle, 1988
Congress, 1989
Mount Rushmore, 1991

Olympic, 1992
Columbus, 1992
World Cup Soccer, 1994
Civil War, 1995
Olympic Torch Runner, 1995
Olympic Stadium, 1995

Coin Sets
Olympic, 1983–84, 1988, 1992, 1995
Statue of Liberty, 1986
Constitution, 1987
Congress, 1989
Mount Rushmore, 1991
Columbus Quincentenary, 1992
Madison/Bill of Rights, 1993
World War II, 1993
World Cup Soccer, 1994
U.S. Veterans, 1994
Civil War, 1995

Chapter 9

RARITIES

In 1894, Superintendent J. Daggett of the San Francisco Mint ordered 24 dimes in proof (the highest quality coin) to be struck for friends. He saved three for his daughter, Hallie. He cautioned her not to spend them because they would be valuable some day. But the thought of a dish of ice cream was too much temptation for Hallie, and she spent one of the dimes immediately. (Wisely, she kept the other two.)

An 1894-S dime; only 14 of these coins are known, making them among the rarest—and most valuable—U.S. coins.

Today, the 1894-S (San Francisco) dime is one of the rarest U.S. coins—only 14 of the 24 have been located. Hallie paid the equivalent of $145,000 for her dish of ice cream, for that's what one of the dimes brought at a 1980 auction. In 1990, one of the dimes brought $275,000.

Although the U.S. is a newcomer in the numismatic history of the world, it has some outstanding rare coins.

Even though the Brasher doubloon was never adopted as coinage, it has become one of the most valuable coins in the world.

THE BRASHER DOUBLOON

Perhaps the most famous American rarity is the Brasher doubloon, struck in 1787 by Ephraim Brasher. It was called a doubloon because it weighed about the same as a Spanish doubloon.

The Brasher doubloon is actually considered a pattern rather than a coin. A pattern is a proposed coin, minted in small quantities, but never adopted as an official coin. Brasher was a private coiner and goldsmith competing for the contract to make copper coins for New York State. Although the coins were to be copper, Brasher minted his patterns in gold, perhaps hoping to impress the officials.

Brasher didn't win the contract, but his doubloons have become the most valuable coins in the world. Seven specimens are known. One Brasher doubloon sold for $725,000, one of the highest prices ever paid for a single coin.

KING OF AMERICAN COINS

The 1804 dollar, which some collectors call the "King of American Coins," wasn't struck in 1804. Eight are believed to have been minted as gifts for royalty (including the King of Siam and the Emperor of Japan) in 1834. In 1859, seven more coins were struck for collectors, a practice that would be frowned upon by mint officials today.

The 1804 dollar was actually minted in 1834 and 1859. Only 15 of these coins are known today.

There are 15 known specimens of the 1804 dollar, making it a very rare coin. One of the dollars sold at an auction in 1980 for $522,500.

THE TRADE DOLLAR

One of the most short-lived U.S. coins was the Trade dollar. Some collectors don't consider it a regular U.S. Mint issue. Trade coins are traditionally struck to be used outside the boundaries of the country in which they are issued. The U.S. Trade dollar was no exception, although it was also legal tender in the United States.

Uncle Sam was looking toward the Pacific and beyond for possible colonization, so he wanted a coin that could be used for Trade in the Far East. In 1873, the mint began producing the U.S. Trade dollar. The coin didn't last long; the U.S. was too late getting into the market. There were two very popular trade coins already being used in the Far East—the Mexican piece

The United States Trade dollar—a failure on the international market, today it is a collectible rarity.

A 1913 Liberty Head nickel, one of five known pieces.

of eight and the Austrian Maria Theresa *thaler* (called the "fat lady coin" by some). The last Trade dollars were struck just 12 years later, in 1885, and the law authorizing the Trade dollar was repealed in 1887.

THE LIBERTY HEAD NICKEL

The Liberty Head design was being phased out in 1912, but five nickels were struck with the design in 1913. They are believed to be trial pieces struck before designs for the 1913 Indian Head or Buffalo type nickels were ready. The 1913 Liberty Head nickels were never meant for circulation and were never officially released. Some of them have ended up in the hands of collectors. They have sold for as much as $962,500.

There are just a few of the many stories about the coins of the United States, young as it is in numismatic history. Many, many more tales fill the pages of books describing the lore of coins. These books can be so fascinating that some collectors collect only coin books.

Chapter 10

ERROR COINS

Each year the U.S. Mint strikes nearly 20 billion coins to make sure that the nation has an adequate supply. Although mint technicians oversee every step of the coining process, it's impossible to produce 20 billion perfect coins. Problems can occur at any stage of minting, from the dies to the metal planchet on which the coin is struck to the coining press.

This cent was struck from a defective planchet.

Even so, errors are so rare in the coining process that these coins present a challenge to collectors. You might open a roll of new coins from the bank and find that a part of a coin or its design is missing. Even noncollectors set aside these pieces to learn more about them.

Error (or misstruck) coins have become a separate category of collecting. There are error coin reference books, clubs, and dealers. The weekly newspaper *Coin World* carries a section devoted to error coins. New finds in error coins are reported. For instance, this section reported an error in a

Some collectors specialize in error coins. This dime is an example of a clipped planchet.

1988 mint set, uncirculated coins packaged by the mint for collectors. The eagle on the reverse of the 1988 Kennedy half dollar is in an upright position, rather than the normal upside-down position.

It's not just modern error coins that attract collectors to this specialty. Earlier error coins have some interesting problems because minting procedures were not as sophisticated as they are today. For instance, you might see a Connecticut copper coin from the late 1700s that was double struck. This means that the coin has two images on it because the die hit the coin twice.

To specialize in error collecting, one must learn the basics of coin manufacture and its unique language to understand such errors as off-center, filled and rotated dies, double struck, and cuds. All of these terms describe error coins or the minting errors that caused them.

Many things can happen to coins once they leave the mint, but only errors that occur during the actual minting process are worthy of study and collection. Collectors should learn how coins are produced in order to detect legitimate errors. (Mint technicians would cringe at the phrase "legitimate errors.")

Values for collectible error coins range from about one dollar for the most common to hundreds of dollars for the rarest.

A poor mix of metals may have caused the flaking and peeling on this coin. This type of defect is called lamination.

A filled die caused this error. When grease or other debris is trapped in the coin die, it prevents parts of the design from being transferred to the coin.

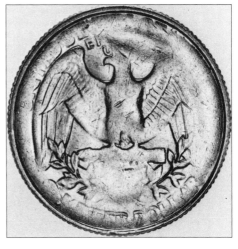

Chapter 11

CANADIAN COINS

A collector who appreciates beautiful, well-struck coins—with designs ranging from dignified English royalty to beavers, bears, and wolves, from geese to ships and from totem poles to prairie flowers—should look to Canada.

A study of Canada's coinage can lead in many directions because of the country's complex history, beginning with French explorer Jacques Cartier's discovery of the Gulf of St. Lawrence in 1534.

This cent shows Canada's national symbol—the maple leaf.

Canadian dollar with portrait of Queen Elizabeth II on the obverse and a Canada goose on the reverse.

EARLY CANADIAN MONEY

Canada, like the United States, had early primitive money and money of necessity. Wampum, tobacco, knives, chisels, dog bells, arrowheads, furs (especially beaver), and even hand-written notes on the backs of playing cards were all used as money in the late 1600s, when Canada was called New France.

Fifty-cent piece with the coat of arms of Canada.

When the French settled Quebec City in 1608, they used French coinage. Near the end of the century, Louis XIV decreed that there would be coins for the French colonies, silver pieces with denominations of five and fifteen *sols*. Colonial coins and French coins were both used until the British gained control in 1763.

Coins then became scarce. Whatever could be found was used, a mixture of gold, silver, and copper coins from Spain, France, England, Ireland, and America. Some people imported tokens from Europe. The local governments began to issue their own tokens, some with and some without British authority. Even banks issued tokens; for example, the Bank of Montreal issued tokens called *Bouquet Sous*, most of which were struck in New Jersey. Canada's colonial coinage was used right up to the beginning of the 20th century in some rural areas.

THE ROYAL CANADIAN MINT

Canada has not always had its own mint. Its official coins were struck in England until 1908, when the Ottawa branch of the British Royal Mint was opened. This became the Royal Canadian Mint in 1931.

The Royal Canadian Mint, a licensed corporation with minimal government supervision, has a reputation for quality coins and innovative programs. Its popular Maple Leaf bullion coin, first introduced in 1979, received immediate worldwide acceptance.

A 1987 Canadian dollar with canoe design.

Nature and outdoor themes dominate Canadian coin designs, as on this five-cent piece with beaver design (left) and ten-cent piece with schooner design.

The mint actively markets its production capacity at its two facilities in Ottawa and Winnipeg. It not only produces Canada's coins, but also has contracts to produce coins for many other countries that have no mints. Its officials know the importance of coin collectors, and they have offered collector coins in sets since 1950. They also actively participate in numismatic activities in both Canada and the United States.

CANADIAN COLLECTORS

Canada has a national organization, the Canadian Numismatic Association (CNA), and many regional coin clubs (see "For More Information," p. 100).

Americans collect Canadian coins, join numismatic organizations north of the border, and serve on the CNA executive committee. In turn, Canadians participate in U.S. coin activities. A Canadian numismatic scholar, J. Douglas Ferguson, was president of the American Numismatic Association in the 1940s. John Jay Pittman of Rochester, New York, an equally esteemed numismatist, served as CNA president from 1969 to 1971 (more proof that numismatics knows no boundaries!).

Canada has excellent money museums, including the national collection at the Bank of Canada in Ottawa. Coin collections for study may be found at several universities and schools. Canada has a National Coin Week each year, as does the United States.

Collectors of Canadian coins, like those who specialize in U.S. coins, enjoy the challenge of collecting by date sequence. Guidebooks and standard catalogs offer historical background, listings, and illustrations of early coins and tokens, government issues, commemoratives, specimen sets, and mintages.

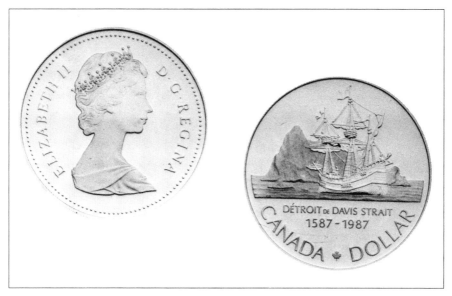

This dollar commemorates the discovery of the Davis Strait in 1587 by explorer John Davis during his unsuccessful attempt to find the Northwest Passage to the Orient.

COMMEMORATIVES

Canada produces some handsome commemorative coins. Commemorative silver dollars celebrate historic occasions in the lives of British rulers. There are dollars to commemorate the silver jubilee of King George V, a Canadian visit by King George VI and Queen Elizabeth, and the silver jubilee of Queen Elizabeth II. (The portrait of Elizabeth II on Canadian coins has been changed over the years, from a young queen to a mature monarch.) The Canadian Olympic commemoratives, beginning in 1973, have exciting designs and are widely collected.

RARITIES

Like the United States., Canada has its share of numismatic rarities. Only three pattern 1911 dollars in silver are known to exist. One of these coins sold for $160,000 in an auction. Other rarities include the 1921 50-cent piece, the 1921 five-cent piece, the 1936 dot cent and 10-cent pieces, and the 1880 gold $2 piece from Newfoundland.

Chapter 12

COINS AS INVESTMENTS

Henry J. Forman, a Philadelphia coin dealer and student of the coin market, knows countless stories about rare coin deals and how they have yielded large profits. One of his favorite stories, however, does not involve a high-priced rarity. He likes to tell how in July 1954 he purchased a U.S. Proof set for $2.10 from the United States Mint. He still owns it. Today it is worth $77, more than 35 times what he paid for it.

Coins can be big business. A collector who puts together coins in choice condition over a period of time gains in satisfaction, and is likely to gain financially as well; statistics show that a collection of quality coins will appreciate in value.

Some increases in value can be spectacular. Q. David Bowers, a professional numismatist, scholar, and prolific author, advertised in 1955 to sell an uncirculated 1907 Saint-Gaudens high-relief gold piece. His price for the coin in 1955 was $145. Today such a coin is worth between $7,100 and $22,500 (perhaps even more), depending upon its condition.

In his 1975 book *Collecting Rare Coins for Profit*, Bowers traced the prices of selected U.S. coins from 1946 to 1974. He found startling percentages of increase in value over that 28-year span—some coins were worth as much as 239 times more in 1974 than they were in 1946.

A comparison of some 1946 prices listed in Bowers' book with 1996 prices for the same coins show that the value of coins continues to increase. The 1996 prices are from *Coin World*, whose weekly "Trends" section is often called the "Dow Jones of the coin market." Today's grading standards are more precise than those in 1946, so there is a range of possible 1996 prices for a coin listed in top condition in 1946. And each increase in grade means a giant step in the coin's value.

In 1946 a 1910 quarter eagle ($2.50 gold piece) in proof was worth $20. Today the same piece is worth $5,700. A 1910 Indian Head eagle ($10 gold piece) was worth $50 in 1946. Today it is valued at $4,900.

A 1937 Indian Head or Buffalo type proof nickel is worth $45. In 1946 you could buy one for $5. A 1942 Mercury dime graded MS-65 could be bought for $1.25 in 1946. It now sells for $6,600. And a Washington quarter from the same year was priced at $2 in 1946. Today it can bring $145.

It's increases like this that attract investors to the coin market. An interesting thing happens to many of these investors. Once they discover that they can combine the pleasure and challenge of a relaxing hobby with their investment, they become serious collectors. They are as interested in the coins themselves as they are in the financial gain the coins might bring.

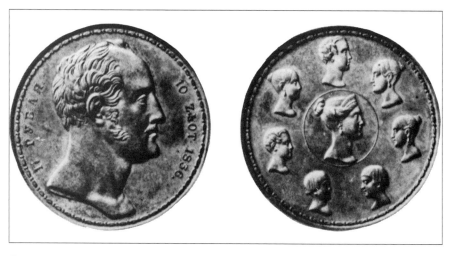

Coin with a family portrait: This one-and-a-half-ruble coin shows Tsar Nicholas I of Russia on the obverse; on the reverse is his wife, Tsaritsa Alexandra Fedorovna, and their seven children.

THE KEYS TO INVESTING

The keys to collecting coins with investment potential are knowledge and patience. If you collect the right coins in good condition and hold on to them for the right amount of time, your investment is very likely to reward you.

The value of a coin is determined by many factors: price trends, intrinsic value (the value of the actual metal in the coin), mintage figures (to determine a coin's rarity), availability, and, above all, the coin's grade (its physical state). As you learn about these things you will be better able to select good investment coins.

Reputable coin firms have investment programs. They will work with potential investors who know little or nothing about coins, helping them to select coins that may appreciate in price. There is no substitute, however, for your own knowledge.

The other key element in coin investment is patience. As you find good investment coins, be prepared to hold on to them. Many collectors recommend that you keep investment coins for at least five years (some say three years) in order to get the best value for them.

Most of all, enjoy the challenge and fun of collecting.

These beautiful porcelain gambling tokens, issued in Siam about 1850, were used as money until the government outlawed them. Some collectors specialize in collecting tokens and other unofficial "coins."

GLOSSARY

Alloy A combination of more than one metal.

Authentication Confirmation by a coin expert that a coin is genuine.

Bit Popular term for Spanish-American one-reale; often used in the plural (two bits, four bits, etc.).

Bronze An alloy made of copper and tin.

Buffalo nickel Another name for the Indian Head five-cent piece, minted in the U.S. 1913–1938.

Bullion (BULL-yun) Uncoined precious metals in bars, plates, and ingots; or a precious metal coin.

Clad Metal strip for coinage using a composite of metals.

Coin A piece of metal issued by a governing authority, marked with a device, and intended to be used as money.

Collar A ring-shaped piece of machinery in a coin press. The collar holds the planchet while it is struck and maintains the round shape of the coin.

Colonials Coins issued by the 13 British colonies before they declared their independence as the United States.

Commemoratives Coins issued to honor a person, place, or event.

Cud A raised blob of metal on a coin caused by a die break at the rim.

Current   Coins in circulation.

Denomination   Face value of a coin.

Device   The main element of a coin design.

Die   A piece of metal, containing the design of a coin in reverse, used to strike coins.

Disme   The way the first U.S. coiners spelled "dime."

Double eagle   A U.S. $20 gold coin.

Double struck   Coins with two images. Caused when the coin rotates between strikes and stays within the collar.

Double die   A die that creates multiple images on a coin.

Doubloon   Spanish eight-escudo piece, often found in pirate treasure.

Eagle   A U.S. $10 gold coin.

Edge   The thin side of a coin; the surface that is neither front nor back.

Electrum   Gold and silver alloy that occurs naturally; used for ancient coins.

Encapsulation   A process of sealing coins and their grading information in a plastic holder for protection. Some collectors call these holders "slabs."

Error   A coin that shows a mistake in its production.

Filled dies   Dies whose recesses are filled with foreign material, resulting in coins with weak or missing designs.

Half eagle   A U.S. $5 gold coin.

Hammered coin   A coin produced by one or more hammer blows on a piece of metal between two dies. Coins were made this way from ancient times until the Renaissance.

Hoard   A hidden deposit of old coins.

Intrinsic   Net metallic value of coins.

Lamination   Defect in coins caused by inferior metal or stress; metal will peel or chip off the coin's surface.

Legend   Inscription on a coin.

Maria Theresa thaler   Austrian silver trade coin dated 1780 but produced with the same date for years.

Medieval coin   A coin struck from about A.D. 500 to 1500.

Mint mark   A symbol or letter indicating the location of the mint where the coin was struck.

Mint set   A set of uncirculated coins packaged by the mint, containing one or each type coin produced in a certain year.

Model   Plaster or clay design for a coin.

Money   Coins, currency, another means of exchange.

Numismatics (noo-miz-MAT-iks)   The science and study of coins, tokens, and objects used as money.

Numismatist   An expert in numismatics.

Obverse   The side of a coin that shows the principal design.

Off-center   A coin that was partly positioned outside of the dies when it was struck. An off-center coin is not perfectly round and part of the design is missing from the surface.

Pattern   A proposed coin of a new design, metal, or denomination that is not adopted during the year it is prepared. Patterns are usually minted in small quantities.

Pieces of eight   Spanish eight-reale pieces.

Pioneer gold   See Territorial coins.

Planchet   Disc of metal on which dies of the coin are impressed.

Proof   The highest quality coin; struck on specially prepared planchets and presses for collectors.

Proof set   A set containing one proof coin of each denomination issued by a mint during a specific year.

Quarter eagle   A U.S. $2.50 gold coin.

Rarity   A scarce coin.

Red Book   Popular name for *A Guide Book of United States Coins,* a standard reference filled with coin information and prices.

Reverse   The back of a coin.

Rim   Raised border around the circumference of a coin.

Rotated dies   A minting error in which the dies are positioned wrong, so that the obverse and reverse designs on the coin do not align at 180 degrees.

Series   Coins of the same denomination, design, and type.

Sestertius (se-STERSH-ee-us)   An ancient Roman coin.

Shekel (SHEK-ul)   A coin of ancient Judea.

Slab   Nickname for an encapsulated coin.

Stater (STATE-er)   An ancient gold or silver Greek coin.

Territorial coins   Gold coins privately produced in the U.S. during the 1800s and used in areas where official coins were scarce. Also called pioneer gold.

Tetradrachm (TET-ra-dram)   An ancient Greek silver coin.

Trade dollar   A coin produced for overseas markets.

Trends   Current market values based on a cross-section of coin transactions.

Type set   A collection containing one of each coin of a given series or period.

Uncirculated set   Set of coins issued by a mint containing one of each coin issued for circulation in a specific year. Also called a mint set.

Unique   Only one specimen known.

Want list   A list prepared by a collector for a dealer describing coins wanted for his or her collection.

Widow's mite   Ancient Jewish lepton, a coin from time of Christ.

Year set   A privately packaged set of coins for one year containing one coin from circulation from each mint.

FOR MORE
INFORMATION

BOOKS

The slogan "first the book and then the coin" means more today than ever. Numismatic books offer prices, information, history, and folklore about coins and collectors. Some people find books about coins so interesting that they specialize in collecting them.

A few of the standard reference books may be found in your local bookstore. Coin shops usually stock a good selection of numismatic books. Your local library may carry some titles or be able to order them from other libraries. Many local coin clubs have their own libraries. Members of the American Numismatic Association may borrow books by mail from the ANA library.

Numismatic book dealers are another good source. The major dealers offer auctions by mail on books and catalogs several times a year. These sales are advertised well in advance in numismatic publications. It can be fun to bid on a book or catalog and wait to see if the bid is accepted. Book dealers offer suggested bids, so you will be able to tell if the item is in your price range. One can build a library easily and reasonably from these sources.

BASIC REFERENCES

The following list contains some basic, readily available books that are affordable on a beginning collector's budget.

America's Gold Coinage. New York: American Numismatic Society, 1990.

America's Silver Coinage, 1796–1891. New York: American Numismatic Society, 1987.

The Charlton Standard Catalogue of Canadian Coins. Toronto: W. K. Cross, 1996.

Coin Collector's Survival Manual. Scott A. Travers. New York: Bonus Books, 1996.

Coin World Almanac. Coin World Editors. Sidney, OH: Amos Press, 1990.

Coins and Collectors. Q. David Bowers. Wolfeboro, NH: Bowers & Merena Galleries, 1964; reprinted 1988.

Comprehensive Catalog & Encyclopedia of United States Coins. Coin World. Sidney, OH: Amos Press, 1995.

A Guide Book of United States Coins. R. S. Yoeman. Racine, WI: Western Publishing Co., annual.

A Guide to the Grading of United States Coins. Brown and Dunn. First edition 1958. Reprinted Racine, WI: Western Publishing Co.

The Handbook of United States Coins. R. S. Yeoman. Racine, WI: Western Publishing Co., annual

Introduction to Numismatics, Grading Coins Today, correspondence courses, American Numismatic Association, Colorado Springs, CO 1995.

Money: History in Your Hands, video, James Earl Jones, narrator; Professional Numismatists Guild, American Numismatic Association, Colorado Springs, CO 1995.

The Money Story, video, curriculum guide, United States Mint, Washington, D.C.

Official ANA Grading Standards for United States Coins. Ken Bressett, A. Kosoff, and Q. David Bowers. Colorado Springs, CO: American Numismatic Association, 1987.

Studies on Money in Early America. Eric P. Newman and Richard G. Doty. New York: American Numismatic Society, 1976.

AN IDEAL LIBRARY

If a coin collector were stranded on the proverbial desert island, the books on the following list would be most welcome. This ideal library contains books that are readily available, as well as books that are out of print or more difficult to find. Check your public library, or a numismatic library if you have access to one.

Some of these classic books are more expensive than those on the list of basic references, but like good coins many can be considered investments.

Adventures with Rare Coins. Q. David Bowers. Los Angeles: Bowers & Ruddy Galleries, 1979.

The Coin Makers. Thomas V. Becker. New York: Doubleday & Co., 1969.

Coins of the World. R. A. G. Carson. New York: Harper & Row, 1962.

Collecting Rare Coins for Profit. Q. David Bowers. New York: Harper & Row, 1975.

Collecting World Coins. Colin Bruce. Iola, WI: Krause Publications, 1994.

Commemorative Coins of the United States. Anthony Swiatek, Coin World. Sidney, OH: Amos Press, 1993.

The Early Coins of America. Sylvester S. Crosby. Boston: New England Numismatic and Archaeological Society, 1873.

The Fantastic 1804 Silver Dollar. Eric P. Newman and Kenneth E. Bressett. Racine, WI: Western Publishing Co., 1972.

First United States Mint. Frank H. Stewart. First edition 1924. Reprinted Lawrence, MA: Quarterman Publications, 1974.

History of the National Numismatic Collections. V. Clain-Stefanelli. Washington, D.C.: Smithsonian Institution Division of Numismatics, 1968.

The Macmillan Encyclopedia Dictionary of Numismatics. Richard G. Doty. New York: Macmillan Publishing Co., 1982.

Numismatics, An Ancient Science. Elvira Clain-Stefanelli. Washington, D.C.: Smithsonian Institution Division of Numismatics, 1965.

Photograde. J. F. Ruddy. First printing 1970. Reprinted Wolfeboro, NH: Bowers & Merena, 1988.

Silver Dollars & Trade Dollars of the United States. Q. David Bowers. Wolfeboro, NH: Bowers and Merena Galleries, 1993.

Standard Catalog of World Coins. Iola, WI: Krause Publications, 1995.

The U.S. Mint and Coinage. Don Taxay. New York: Arco Publishing Co., 1966.

Walter Breen's Complete Encyclopedia of U.S. and Colonial Coins. New York: F.C.I. Press/Doubleday, 1988.

World War II Remembered—History In Your Hands. C. Frederick Schwan and Joseph E. Boling, Port Clinton, OH: BNR Press, 1995.

PERIODICALS

The editors of each of these publications want to help new collectors learn about the hobby. They will gladly furnish information and sample copies.

WEEKLY NEWSPAPERS

Coin World, P.O. Box 150, Sidney, OH 45365

Numismatic News Weekly, Iola, WI 54990

MONTHLY MAGAZINES

COINage Magazine, 2660 East Main Street, Ventura, CA 93003

Coins Magazine, Iola, WI 54990

The Numismatist, American Numismatic Association, 818 North Cascade Avenue, Colorado Springs, CO 80903

QUARTERLY MAGAZINE

First Strike, American Numismatic Association, 919 North Cascade Avenue, Colorado Springs, CO 80903 (For young numismatists.)

Collector Organizations

National numismatic organizations offer many services to collectors. Both American organizations have museums and libraries. The American Numismatic Association will lend books by mail to its members.

There are many national specialty organizations, as well as hundreds of regional, state, and local coin clubs. For more information about coin clubs in your area, ask a local dealer or write to one of the national organizations listed here.

American Numismatic Association, 818 North Cascade Avenue, Colorado Springs, CO 80903

American Numismatic Society, Broadway at 155th Street, New York, NY 10032-7598

Canadian Numismatic Association, P.O. Box 226, Barrie, Ontario, L4M 4T2, Canada

Major Mints Around the World

Here are addresses for some of the world's major mints. If you write to them, you should ask for a list or catalog of collector coins and prices. They may refer you to a distributor in the United States. Most U.S. dealers in world coins advertise in coin publications. The Treasury/United States Mint's Money Story video and curriculum guide are free but require $4.50 for handling and postage. To be placed on the U.S. Mint's customer mailing list or to receive information on current coin offerings, write: United States Mint, Customer Service Center, 10001 Aerospace Road, Lanham, MD 20706.

Australia
Royal Australian Mint
Denison Street, Deakin
2600 ACT, Australia

Belgium
Monnaie royale de Belgique
32, Boulevard Pacheco
1000 Bruxelles, Belgium

Canada
Royal Canadian Mint
320 Sussex Drive
Ottawa, Ontario K1A 0G8, Canada

China
Printing and Mint Bureau
People's Bank of China, No. 3
Xi Jie, Bai Zhi Fang
Xuan Wu District
Beijing, People's Republic of China

Colombia
Banco de la Republica
Casa de Moneda-Ibaghe
Cra. 7 n2 14-78
Bogota, Colombia

Denmark
Den Kongelige Mont
Solmarksvej 5
2605 Brondby, Denmark

Finland
Suomen Rahapaja
Mint of Finland
Suometsantie 1
SF-01741 Vantaa Finland

France
Administration des Monnaies et
    Medailles
11, quai de Conti
75006 Paris, France

Germany
Mune Berlin
Molkenmarkt 1-3
0-1020 Berlin, Germany

Greece
Bank of Greece
Messogion Str. 341, Halandri
15231 Athens, Greece

India
India Government Mint
Shahid Bhagatsingh Road
Bombay 400 023 India

Ireland
Central Bank of Ireland
Currency Centre
Sandyford, Dublin 16, Ireland

Israel
Bank of Israel
P.O. Box 780
91007 Jerusalem, Israel

Italy
Italia "La Zecca"
Via Principe Umberto 4
00185 Roma, Italy

Japan
Mint Bureau, Ministry of Finance
1–1–79, Kita-ku
530 Osaka, Japan

Mexico
Casa de Moneda de Mexico
Paseo de la Reforma, No. 295–50, piso
Col. Cuauhtemoc, 06500, Mexico, D.F.

Netherlands
Dutch Mint
Leidseweg 90
P.O. Box 2407
3531 BG Utrecht, Netherlands

Norway
Den Kongelige Mynt
Hyttegaten 1
P.O. Box 53
N–3601 Kongsberg, Norway

Poland
Polish State Mint
Pereca 21
00–950 Warsaw, Poland

Portugal
Imprensanacional, Casa de Moeda
Av. Antonio Jose de Almeida
1000 Lisbon, Portugal

Republic of Korea
Korea Security Printing and Minting
  Corp.
35 Kajong-dong, Yusong-Gu
Taejon, 305–350, Korea

Republic of Russia
Moscow Mint
Podolsk Ave. 1
113093 Moscow, Russia

Singapore
Singapore Mint Pte Ltd.
249 Jalan Boon Lay
2261 Singapore

South Africa
South African Mint
P.O. Box 464
0001 Pretoria, South Africa

Spain
Fabrica Nacional de Moneda y Timbre
Jorge Juan, 106
28009 Madrid, Spain

Sweden
AB Tumba Bruk Swedish Mint
S-147 82 Tumba, Sweden

Switzerland
Federal Administration of Finances
Swiss Federal Mint, Bernerhof
Berne CH 3003, Switzerland

Thailand
Treasury Department
Rama VI Road
10400 Bangkok, Thailand

Turkey
Turkish State Mint
Emirhan Cad-Yildiz
Darphane Mudurlugu
Istanbul, Turkey

United Kingdom
British Royal Mint
Llantrisant, Pontyclun
CF7 8 YT Mid Glamorgan
United Kingdom

United States
United States Mint
10001 Aerospace Road
Lanham, MD 20706

INDEX

error, 85–87
factors determining value of, 94
grades and rarity of, 51
grading standards of, 93
how to hold, 56
how to make, 59–74
as investments, 92–95
metals used in, 31
of Middle Ages, 31–32
rare, 81–84
round, introduction of, 25
storing, 56–58
collectors
Canadian, 90
contemporary, 13–14
ethics of, 54
organizations of, 13
young, 14–15
Colonial coins, 35–36
Columbian Exposition commemorative, 75
Confederacy, currency of, 41
Confucius, 26
copper crosses, 21
copper disme, 37
counterfeiting, 60, 61
cowrie shell, 18
Croesus, 25

Daggett, J., 81
Davis Strait, 91
dealers, 16, 53–54
decadrachm, 75
deep-sea treasure finds, 14
Diehl, Phillip N., 59
Diderot, Denis, 62
dies, 59–60, 63–67
  filled, 86–87
disme, 37
distater, 29
Dobson, Henry Austin, 23
dog tooth money, 21
dollar. *See also specific names*
  Canadian, 88, 90, 91
  1804, 83
  origin of term, 31, 32
  Trade, 83–84
double eagle, 47

eagle, 47
Edward VIII pattern crown, 53
Egyptians, 18
Eisenhower dollar, 42, 72
Elizabeth II, Queen, 91
encapsulated holders, 57, 58
engraving, 71–72
error coins, 85–87
Eskimos, money of, 22

Far East, primitive money from, 19
Ferguson, J. Douglas, 90
Forman, Harry J., 92
Franklin, Benjamin, 36
Franklin cent, 36
Franklin half dollar, 70
Fugio cent, 36

Gasparro, Frank, 43
George V, King, 91
George VI, King, 91
gold eagle, 47, 67
gold rings, 18
gold rush, 39–40
grades, 51, 93, 94
Greek coins, ancient, 11, 23, 27–28, 75
Greek gods, 27–28
Greeks, ancient, 11
guidebooks, 49, 54, 90
guildiner, 31
gulden groschen, 32

half disme, 37
half eagle, 47
Hercules, 27
history, in coined, 11–12
hogge money, 35
Hull, John, 35

incuse dies, 60
Indian Head half eagle, 47
Indian Head nickel, 93
"In God We Trust" motto, 36
intaglio dies, 60
International Primitive Money Society, 22
investments, 92–95
iron bars, 21

Isabella, Queen, 76
ivory, 21

jade coins, 19
Japan, gold and silver coins of, 26
Jefferson nickel, 70, 71, 72
Jewish coins, ancient, 30–31
Joachimsthaler, 31, 32
Jones, Elizabeth, 41, 71
Jupiter, 27, 28
Justinian II, Emperor, 30

Kennedy, John F., 43
Kennedy half dollar, 33, 42–43, 70, 86
"Key" money, 18
King of American Coins, 83
kissi penny, 20
knife money (tao), 19

lamination defect, 87
Liberty Head nickel, 84
Lovett, Robert, Jr., 40
Lydia, 24–25

Macedonia, 27
Maesa, Julia, 29
magnifying glass, 50
mail order transactions, 53
manillas, 21
Maria Theresa thaler, 84
Mercanti, John, 71
Mercury dime, 93
Middle Ages, coins of, 31–32
mint marks, 69–71
minting. *See* coinmaking
misstruck coins. *See* error coins
money. *See also* coins
  with a soul, 20
  earliest, 17–22
  materials used for, 21
  primitive, 22
"money trees," 19
museums, 13, 90

Native American money, 22, 34
Near East, primitive money from, 18
Nero, Emperor, 29

ABOUT THE AUTHOR

Margo Russell spent 25 years with the weekly newspaper *Coin World* and had a strong hand in building it into a successful hobby publication. Although Mrs. Russell retired as editor of the newspaper in 1986, she continues to work for the good of the hobby.

During her *Coin World* career, Mrs. Russell often testified before Congress on behalf of collectors. She served as a member of many federal advisory committees on coins, including the American Revolution Bicentennial coins and medals panel.

A frequent lecturer on coins and medals, Mrs. Russell has traveled extensively. She has studied coins in Israel and has toured Europe as a numismatic ambassador, meeting with collectors and mint officials in Eastern Europe.

She is a member of major numismatic organizations in the United States and abroad, and is a councillor of the American Numismatic Society in New York.

Mrs. Russell was elected to the American Numismatic Association's Hall of Fame in 1986, and holds its highest honor, the Farran Zerbe award.

If you enjoyed *Start Collecting Coins*
try *Start Collecting Stamps*,
also available from Running Press.